LIVING BY CHOICE

LIVING
BY
CHOICE

The Theory and Practice of Self-Determination

by
Donald J. Tyrell

PHILOSOPHICAL LIBRARY
NEW YORK

Library of Congress Catalog Card No. 77-075260
SBN 8022-2205-6

Manufactured in the United States of America

For Barbara

and

Paul and Karen.

INTRODUCTION

Donald Tyrell has written a hopeful book. By stressing that our mental health is subject to choices, he frees us from the danger of fatalism. We tend to believe that feelings and emotions have such deep roots that they escape our decision making. When confronted with low self-esteem, fear, anger, depression, or anxiety-provoking sexual feelings, we quite often say to each other or to ourselves: "Accept it and try to live with it". In many respects we have become quite fatalistic with respect to our own lives. The best we can do, we seem to think, is to recognize our often hidden powers and impulses and to befriend them as much as possible. Sometimes we even seem to think that our task is to discover who we really are and then live within the limits of our discovery.

I know people who are so fascinated by their own psychological make up that they relate to themselves as to interesting puzzles which, once put together in the right way, will show them clearly their own "real picture" and indicate to them how to live. With a certain happy pride they say: "Well I am an angry type; Well I am a dependent person; Well I am a melancholic personality; Well I am a homosexual", implying all the time that this is their good or bad fate which must be obeyed.

The importance of Tyrell's contribution is that he unmasks this illusion and restores the concept of "choice" in the healing process. Choice rather than accommodation occupies the central place in his psychological perspective. With the help of verbatim reports of his therapeutic sessions, Tyrell illustrates his conviction that healing takes place when we recognize that the complex of values, goals and behavior which causes our pains is the result of a series of choices and thus can be altered by new choices.

In restoring choice to the center of the healing process, Tyrell's book is a hopeful book, yet it is not based on a romantic optimism. Tyrell shows clearly the hard and arduous task of self determination. He makes it plain that in order to be able to make healing choices we have to make our own unwanted thoughts and feelings available for decisions which lead to change. This requires much more than "getting over" disquieting feelings. It requires a "living through" them to their roots. Thus the pain which first seemed to debilitate can become the source of creativity and strength.

Tyrell's book is indeed a hopeful book. It restores the precious truth that our lives are really ours.

Henri J. M. Nouwen
Yale University

CONTENTS

Basic Values. Pleasure and Power. The Choice to Care.
Responsibility

Pain. Failure. Frustration. Guilt. Responding to Limits.
The Choice to Hide. Forms of Hiding. Guilt Feelings.
Transforming Limits.

Feelings from the Past. The Lessons of Restraint.
Breaking Patterns. The Roots of Pretense.
Beginning Again.

Experimenting with Imagining. The Nature of
Imagining. Fear of Imagining. The Choice to
Imagine. Therapeutic Imagining.

PROLOGUE

Each of the chapters in this book attempts to relocate freedom of choice in some human context from which it has been dismissed by custom, misunderstanding, or malice. Together they form a psychological point of view about the theory and practice of self-determination which has been over twenty years of clinical experience in the making. In an earlier work *(When Love is Lost*; Waco, Texas: Word Books, 1972), I concentrated my attention on the principles and procedures of what I called at the time Disclosure-Confrontation Therapy and later Self-Determination Therapy. The present book is meant to complement what I did there, both by providing it with a broader framework and by tracing its consequences in some greater detail.

The fundamental premise that informs everything written in these pages is that the proper aim of human existence is not the achievement of liberation from pain, frustration, failure, and guilt, but rather the search for meaning in those limits which our very nature imposes on us. In this way I hope to show that our capacity for living by choice can be fully exercised not only in managing what falls within our understanding and control, but also in accepting responsibility for the unknown and uncontrollable things of our life. This in turn will lead us to conclude that psychotherapy, insofar as it ignores the choices that lie behind human suffering in its effort to help an individual recover peace of mind and body, is itself sadly in need of therapy.

A number of dramatic examples in the form of tape-recorded excerpts from actual group therapy sessions have been included at various points throughout the book. I elected to use this form in place of the more traditional case history whenever I felt it necessary to draw attention to the real, concrete character of the therapeutic process itself. Together with other examples cited, these excerpts represent the contextual footnotes, the practical sources upon which I have relied for the theory presented in the text.

ACKNOWLEDGMENTS

Many persons, knowingly and unknowingly, have contributed to the writing of this book—many more than I could list in a short space.

I wish to acknowledge Joy Neuman for her many professional editorial suggestions, Dr. Thomas Banchoff for his critical reading of earlier drafts of the manuscript, and Carole Wendt, Gay Meier and Dee Uhlmansiek who typed the manuscript through its several drafts.

I owe particular thanks to Dr. Bede Smith for helping with the original draft of two of the chapters, and for undertaking the tedious and demanding task of organizing my often idiosyncratic rush of thoughts into respectable, logical sequence; and to Dr. Jim Heisig who dismantled the text sentence by sentence, from start to finish, and put it back together under the critical eye which is his gift. The ideas are my own responsibility, of course; but without their help it would have been difficult communicating them as I wanted to.

In a real sense this book is theirs as well as mine. Drs. Heisig, Smith and I have worked closely over the years, the roles of teacher and student often overlapping and sometimes unclear. In fact, it was this very point that became the catalyst which drew us together. The clarification of our own thinking, feeling, imagining, and being, we have attempted to express in these pages. The pain, joy, suffering, delight, and excitement of our relationship cannot be expressed in words. We invite our readers to our sentiments as they learn to experience the fullness of life that living by reasonable human choice can produce.

Finally, I am grateful beyond words to my wife Barbara and our two children, Paul and Karen. In dedicating these pages to them, I only wish to return what belongs to them more than to anyone else.

Donald J. Tyrell, Ph.D.

Arlington Heights, Illinois

Living by Choice

CHAPTER ONE

CHOICE

In modern consumer-oriented cultures, man's search for meaning is often made to conform to conditions which all but ensure its very impossibility. The instructional manual is perhaps the literary form which best represents this process. In addition to the whole range of books telling us how to succeed at business, how to invest our capital in the market, and how to repair autos and refrigerators, there are others which offer the secrets of how to succeed at making love, how to invest our feelings in personal relationships, and how to repair marriages and generation gaps. There is even a new spate of manuals on how to get the most out of other manuals. Most of these "how to do it" approaches, while offering something of apparent practical use, cloak a dangerous bias. We are taught *what* to do and *how* to do it, while very little attention is given to *why* we ought to be doing it at all. This seems, in part, the result of a technology that prizes technique and efficiency—in matters both mechanical and human—over an assessment of genuine needs. But the more we identify *searching* with learning how to do things without understanding or questioning why, the more uncritical we become of the *meanings* advertised for our consumption. The pleasure and power we are promised in return remain forever just beyond our grasp: tempting, demanding, enslaving us to their service.

The process of freeing ourselves to search for meanings

made to the measure of our humanity begins with some understanding of our values. Talk about values is, in the first place, talk about what I hold as important and desirable. Those values which I single out as basic relate not only to the things of my life which I consider most essential but also to the goals which I pursue in my activity. Basic values attend both to the question "What about me is most fully me?" and to the question "What am I after in life?" The two questions are by no means unrelated. The way I perceive myself is reflected in the way I direct my behavior, even as my behavior affects the project of coming to understand who I am.

In the second place, then, talk about values is critical to talk about changing behavior. As I come to discover those values that give order and unity to my life and my life-style, I am in a position to affirm or modify the means I use in attaining those ends. In this way, becoming aware of an imbalance in my evaluation of prestige, social status, control or pleasure to the detriment of common sense, social conscience, or healthy self-esteem is preliminary to any abiding change in my patterns of behavior. Changing my goals requires first a change in values. Any educational process which ignores this simple fact is doomed to futility, as the appalling rate of return of those entrusted to our prison systems and mental institutions attests only too well.

BASIC VALUES
At this point it is necessary to clarify what I understand as the basic values indispensible to mature human living. First among them is *truthfulness*, a value often more easily appreciated in its absence than in its presence. The subtle strains of untruthfulness, deceit, and flight from reality—only occasionally surfacing in a deliberate lie—confront us at every step, in our solitude and in social intercourse. Truthfulness

2

involves accepting the fullness of how I perceive things, difficult as that may be. It may be a simple truth that I find hard to accept, or a more complex truth requiring discipline and study. But, like wisdom and genuineness which are its fruits, truthfulness has never been commonplace among men.

The second basic value is *freedom*. Freedom is the capacity and the right to choose a course of action and follow through on it. It entails not merely doing what I can, but learning how best to live in order to maximize my potential. Here, too, awareness of freedom is keenest when it has been lost. When I am kept from doing what I might otherwise have done, when I am no longer able to do things that once came easy, when I am faced with the consequences of a bad choice—at such times I sense best what it is to be free. Freedom cannot be divorced from responsibility: the more one is free *for*, the more is one response-able. Nor should it be confused with spontaneity, which is merely the absence of emotional inhibitions and of itself an unreliable gauge of maturity. Freedom requires rather a truthfulness about available options and their consequences.

The final basic value is *care*. I hesitate to say "love" for fear my meaning would be lost on a word whose conventional definitions often seem to omit the ingredient of care. By care I understand the ability to see another human being as he is, to value his independence of me as *carus*—as dear—and to treat him accordingly. It presupposes the ability to care for myself, to appreciate my own worth and intrinsic dignity. In other words, care begins in truthfulness and is fulfilled in the invitation to freedom.

Truthfulness, freedom, and care—the three values basic to human maturity—are, by their very nature as *values*, open-ended and incomplete. No one of us is ever totally truthful: there is always more to know than we want to, and more that we do know than we can communicate. None of us is ever totally free; physical ability, emotional sensitivity, intellectual insight, and external conditions always limit the reaches of ambition. Nor can we ever be totally caring; our concern is always selective, often inconsistent, and usually painfully less than we aspire to.

On the other hand, as *basic* values, truthfulness, freedom, and care can never be totally absent. We cannot escape our perceptions entirely, cannot relinquish altogether our freedom of choice, cannot repress totally our awareness of the worth of others. At least in some minimal sense, these three values impel us beyond ourselves—to the world about us, to the future ahead of us, to others like us. Taken together they protect us from isolation as we seek to answer the questions "What about me is most fully me?" and "What am I after in life?"

PLEASURE AND POWER

Defining truthfulness, freedom, and care as the values basic to the mature personality enables us to see more clearly the foundations of the immature personality: pleasure and power. As we shall see, the problem is not so much that pleasure and power *replace* the basic values, but rather that they *distort* them, twisting them to goals and forms of behavior which render them ineffective.

An infant lives for pleasure and power. Elementary pleasures of food, warmth, and elimination govern his behavior, as do the elementary discomforts of hunger, cold, rash, and gastric upset. He accepts what is pleasant and rejects what is unpleasant. As long as his basic comfort is maintained, the infant is content, awake or asleep. When it is lost, he registers disapproval by crying. In this way he learns to master his dependency, to overpower the adult world about him with a cunning and efficiency not usually associated with so helpless and weak a creature. When he

4

is hungry, his howls bring mother and milk. When he is cold, the blanket is only a whimper away. When frightened, his wail brings comfort and security. The infant's cry is an altogether effective tool for controlling the behavior of others and bringing about the gratification of his needs.

But soon the day arrives when satisfaction does not come so quickly and he is expected to conform to the wishes of others. Instead of being fed instantly, he must wait for mealtime. A young brother or sister may come along to usurp his privileged position at the center of mother's undivided attention. He is no longer allowed to eliminate as he pleases but is disciplined to the use of the toilet. Once infantile omnipotence has been undermined, the child must learn other ways to protect his pleasures and to cope with the power of others interested in their own needs.

As the child grows older and learns to appreciate the impact which his activity has *on others* besides himself, alternatives to pleasure and power begin to present themselves. He may, of course, choose to ignore these alternatives and cling to his previous patterns of selfishness. But the fact that he is able to imagine the consequences of what he does— remembering what has happened in the past and anticipating that it will happen again—gives a new meaning and weight to his choices. What kind of person the child becomes is now also and irrevocably the result of his own choices.

The transition from pleasure and power to the quest for more basic values to guide behavior depends on growth in self-determination. However, if the small but important choices of childhood continue to be based exclusively on comfort and control, the infantile habits unreflectively acquired may solidify into a style of life carrying over into adulthood. Now while it is necessary for the infant to live for self-gratification, it is infantile for the adult to do so. But the fact is that choices tend to follow the line of least resistance, to form patterns and so to bias behavior into habits. Thus as the range of actions governed by choice increases in the life of the child, learning to discipline activity to goals becomes critical. Such self-determination does not come spontaneously and without effort. How a person develops, once he becomes *able* to make choices of his own by considering possible goals and working towards them, depends on his own effort and how he *in fact* selects goals and directs his energies to achieve them. Unlike the flower that *must* blossom when all the nutrients are present, the human personality does not have to mature, and sometimes does not. Indeed, a person may opt not to take the initiative that would lead him beyond childhood to adulthood.

THE CHOICE TO CARE

As we begin to grow in truthfulness by learning how to imagine the wider consequences of our activities, and as we begin to grow in freedom by learning the discipline of self-determination, so too we begin to integrate truthfulness and freedom with care by recognizing that there are others about us with their own needs and aspirations. We become aware of other persons, each a center to his own life, and learn to value their well-being even as we value our own. We no longer relate to others simply on the basis of our own desires, assuming that they respond to things as we do. We choose to care about them and their independence of us.

Few people have difficulty in accepting care as desirable. The problem comes in translating it into concrete behavior without falling prey to the careless control of others in this less than best of all possible worlds. In this sense, power and pleasure seem more reliable guides to securing our basic needs. And even where we do accept care as a possibility, we discover again and again the many and various ways in

6

which our own immaturity stands in the way. All of which confirms the fact that care is a *choice*, an investment of belief in a value basic to the mature personality. It is a meaning which we seek to grow into, and as such is neither automatic nor without its price. To capitulate to conventional criticism is to confuse the desirable with the possible and to forget those times when we have been touched by care, or so touched others. As with truthfulness and freedom, it is success in care that confirms what is possible, not failure.

From the standpoint of power, other persons are viewed as potential enemies to be controlled, neutralized, or placated. It is the same childhood desire for power that survives and dominates so much of adult life, albeit in a far more sophisticated manner. The child who hoards toys too often becomes the adult who selfishly amasses property and stocks. The child who bullies his playmates becomes the boss who browbeats employees or the political leader who tramples over the rights of minorities. Instead of the infant's tears, the adult uses money, status, sexual favors, or education to get what he wants. A teacher, for instance, may maintain control over his students and enjoy his privileged position of power rather than joining with them on a mutual search for understanding and exposing his insights for their criticism. Each challenge is interpreted as a threat against which the individual must defend himself. As long as the backdrop of human relationships is a battlefield, each side must fight for victory. The success of one demands the failure of another. The strong must dominate the weak and the weak must placate the strong.

The survival of childhood preoccupations with pleasure into adult life is somewhat more complex. What remains constant, however, is the criterion of what is desirable: what is comfortable, what is fun, what registers the greatest approval with others, what brings the richest rewards for the least effort. Where such a principle dominates, the loftier

7

aspirations we identify with the mature personality are discarded in favor of immediate gratification. Like power, pleasure has as its final point of reference the isolated, uncaring self.

Care can begin to displace power and pleasure only when the self ceases to be *the* center of its own interests and affections and becomes *one* center among many. Care seeks its completion in relationships of love, which alone can cast out fear of declining power and pleasure. And the fullness of such love is what we mean when we say we trust in God as our Father. For the man of faith, to name God as Love is the final guarantee for the standpoint of care which he chooses as the basis of his relationship to other men.

RESPONSIBILITY

It would be shortsighted to conclude at this point that the desire for power and pleasure is altogether reprehensible and immature. To be sure, if left unchecked, in their infantile forms, power and pleasure tend to distort our basic values to selfish ends. But, on the other hand, the attempt to integrate truthfulness, freedom, and care into a style of life would be unthinkable without some responsible appropriation of power and pleasure as well. To suppose otherwise would be to define maturity in terms of a radical break with infancy and childhood and to deprive our basic values of their human context.

To view pleasure and power as necessary is not thereby to adopt them as sufficient guides for behavior. An ethic of pleasure is not the only alternative to a puritanical repression of everything pleasant any more than an ethic of power is the only alternative to blind submissiveness. Our basic values provide us with an appropriate perspective for pleasure and power, and that is indeed their principal function. Our choices on the basis of those values determine the

8

responsible integration of pleasure and power into behavior.

The insistance that we live by the values we choose, therefore, establishes responsibility as the mark of the mature personality. Responsibility accepts with pride accomplishments following upon reasoned choices, just as it accepts with repentance failures following upon unreasoned choices. Responsibility embraces the search for meaning in life and resolutely refuses to hand it over to another.

CHAPTER TWO

LIMITS

Some of the most important choices of a lifetime are those a person makes in the face of limits.

At first sight, this statement sounds contradictory, since limit and choice seem to be mutually exclusive terms. Insofar as I am limited, I cannot choose; and insofar as I have a choice, there are no limits.

The first step towards understanding the paradox is to realize that man is a being who can help to create the experience of his own limits by his exercise of imagination. His imagination continually outreaches his actual capacities. He can set himself goals which he will not, even cannot, reach. A man experiences limits to his endeavors in a way that the animal does not simply because of the sheer volume of productivity of his imagination. And so it is that man's most distinctive characteristic—imagining possibilities—seems to contain within itself the assurance of ever greater happiness.

In order better to appreciate how the choices we make can transcend and transform the creative power of imagination, let us look in some detail at four limit-experiences familiar to all of us: pain, failure, frustration, and guilt.

PAIN

The first of the limit-experiences to be considered is pain. The actual experience of pain, or hurt, is an unpleasant sensation, a limit to the comfort we desire. This in turn acts

10

as a biological warning system to alert us that something is wrong and we react at once accordingly. When I touch my hand to a hot stove, I spontaneously react by drawing back. Similarly, if someone or something has hurt me badly in the past, my reflex reaction is to keep a safe distance to prevent it from happening again. All of us have known pain to one degree or another, just as all of us depend on our memory of painful experiences to find ways of minimizing their recurrence.

On the other hand, the single-minded effort to avoid all pain at all costs often exacts a heavier price from the total personality than the experiencing of the sharp but transitory pain. An excessive fear of getting hurt—and its concomitant pursuit of pleasure as the only good—eventually leads the subject to further and further alienation from the world of people and things about him.

Let us say I once touched an electric fence and received a painful shock in return. The next time I see an electric fence, I am reminded of what happened and begin to feel frightened, even from a reasonably safe distance. If I simply allow my overreaction to take hold and yet try to ignore the memory of that first experience, it is likely that my fear will only increase with time, to the point where eventually I may shrink away from all wire fences. Or again, let us say that this same pattern is followed after a childhood experience of being ridiculed for making a mistake. In time, as an adult, I may be terrified of expressing my opinion at all in public. Alternatively, I may react with unnecessary anger to things or persons in situations which stir up memories of past painful experiences.

In such cases, fear and anger are protective devices which keep us from repeating unpleasant experiences. But the fear and anger themselves may in turn become unpleasant, so that we want to hide these feelings as well. We learn not to show that we are afraid; we learn not to express our anger.

11

And when this happens, the defense against pain is complete, shielding us not only from all avoidable pain, but also from the responsibility of integrating the meaning of pain as a limit-experience into the fabric of our lives.

FAILURE

A second limit-experience is failure. Like pain, failure is an unavoidable part of life, one which confronts us with the limits of our competence. The ability to do something well only comes gradually as a rule, with practice, and after many mistakes. Performing poorly, however, is an unpleasant experience. Our desire for proficiency aims to overcome that unpleasantness by ensuring that we take the necessary efforts to improve.

But failure is not failure, of course, until I have established some level of proficiency against which to measure my achievement. Failure is the inability to do well according to some standard of excellence, and that makes it a peculiarly human privilege denied animals, who cannot set goals and norms for themselves. By the same token, a person can choose a variety of responses to failure. The individual who sets high goals for himself will experience failure more keenly than one who expects only mediocre performance. By acknowledging failure, however, he opens the possibility of making adjustments either in his goals or in the means adopted to reach them. The fact of failure need not block the desire for proficiency, but neither should it block awareness of limitations brought to light in seeking that proficiency. If an individual judges his failure as an unqualified evil, and fears that he will be hurt if others come to know of it, his mistakes become a deformity to be hidden. To the extent that one's self-esteem is built on success alone, failure is a shattering experience of shame and embarrassment. One feels shame when the failure in performance falls below self-imposed standards and feels embarrassment at being exposed to possible ridicule in the eyes of others. By getting mired in feelings of shame and embarrassment, the individual pulls back from risking the mistakes necessary to progress. This may also lead to the denial of failure, so that one comes to live out a pretense of perfection that one knows is simply not true. When failure is unacknowledged, the gap between pretense and reality can only widen, so that ever greater efforts have to be made to cloak the failure. In short, by choosing to hide the truth about one's ability because it seems safer than facing threats to self-esteem, one is kept from accepting full responsibility for the limit-experience of failure.

FRUSTRATION

A third sense of limits is met in frustration. As failure is the experience of personal incompetence in the face of a chosen goal, frustration is the experience of personal competence kept from its chosen goal by outside interference. The effect is the same: the goal remains alive to imagination but unachieved in reality. The emotional defenses, however, tend to be distinct. Where failure leads to shame and embarrassment, frustration more often provokes anger at the obstacle or rationalizations for passive inactivity. Anger and rationalization are ways of capitulating prematurely to frustration, and so removing the experience of the limit in an irresponsible manner. As more and more attention is awarded the actual interference, less energy and creativity can be directed to seeking an alternate course of action of one's own choosing.

We always remain radically limited by the conditions under which we must set out to achieve the goals we have decided upon. In fact, the more creative one is and the more ambitious one's goals, the more likely one is to en-

13

counter obstacles that cause frustration. In addition to nature's notorious indifference to the best made plans of men, one has always to take into account the various forms of social restriction which—rightly or wrongly—impede achievement.

At the same time, the very creativity which is the source of frustration equips us with a means for coping with it, for accepting responsibility for what natural and social limits have done to us. In other words, understanding frustration enables us better to assess the nature of the obstacle and to seek solutions for its removal; but it also enables us to gain greater insight into the very processes of imagination which help create our sense of limits in the first place.

GUILT

The final limit-experience we shall consider here is guilt, which confronts us with our moral incapacity. Guilt is the awareness of inconsistency between what we hold as valuable and what we in fact value. It is the sense of a breach between what we perceive as desirable and what our actual choices are. As a limit-experience, guilt is a rational judgment about the relationship between moral norms and moral behavior.

Like failure and frustration, guilt reminds us of goals unrealized. But whereas failure discloses objective limitations of competence, and whereas frustration points to limiting circumstances in the external environment, guilt reveals a lack of personal conviction, a disorder in the internal environment. Fear and frustration threaten us with fears of impotence. Guilt threatens us with the fear of being evil, of lacking moral fibre, of behaving out of harmony with the ideals we profess.

14

The possible defenses an individual may erect to systematize his neglect of guilt are almost endless. They cover everything from purely ritualized forms of repentance to giving way to feelings of worthlessness and nursing resentment again oneself. What is common to all such defenses is the avoidance of change. Ironically, the most subtle form of denying guilt is harboring guilt feelings, which shall be discussed in greater detail later on. For the moment, suffice it to say that accepting guilt as a limit-experience entails examining the disharmony exposed and assuming the responsibility of adjusting either behavior or values accordingly.

Responding To Limits
Because limit-experiences are conscious to the human being in a way they are not to the animal, he need not simply follow the force of instinct in responding to them. He can make choices which will be self-destructive or choices which will be self-esteeming. This was implicit in the brief treatment of the four examples singled out for the study of limits. At this point, it is necessary to make explicit the distinct types of responses available in the face of limit-experiences.

In the first place, one can *react* to a limit. Reaction is the simplest response of all: it is the choice *not to choose*. Reaction is the reflex away from the limit and into hiding. It is self-destructive in the long run, because it is an avoidance of the truth about the conditions which define self-determination. By putting a premium on escape from pain, an individual denies the experience any possible meaning. In time, the fear and anger protecting this withdrawal fall into the same pattern and are hidden away behind more comfortable forms of response. Likewise, the embarrassment and shame that help us to disguise failure are eventually disguised themselves. The reflex reactions to frustration, especially passivity and anger, not only screen us from our limitations but arrange for their own justification. Reactions against accepting responsibility for guilt tend to become stabilized in the form of pretenses to moral harmony. In each case hiding marks the reactionary and self-defeating choice not to respond creatively to the experience of a limit.

In the second place, a person can respond to a limit by *accepting* its truth as part of his experience. He can accept pain and hurt, neither pretending that they do not exist nor simply striving to avoid them. He can acknowledge failure and live with the consequences of his shortcomings. He can meet obstacles without withdrawing or abandoning his goal. He can take responsibility for his moral behavior, sorting out his moral ideals, trying to live in ways that are consistent with them, and accepting guilt wherever it confronts him. Limit-experiences do not need to be sought out; but neither do they need to be repressed when they occur, as they inevitably do, through the course of life.

Finally, a person can *creatively transform* the limits of a situation and so complete the response begun in acceptance. Once accepted as a reality, pain can be appropriated into the meaning which an individual gives his life. In this way, pain can be viewed as relative in terms of one's basic values, and it can also render one more empathetic to the suffering of others. Similarly, failures can become opportunities for learning, and frustration can lead to a responsible transformation of the limiting conditions impeding activity. Guilt, once acknowledged for what it is, can be incorporated into the person's search for value-informed behavior. In short, creative transformation is the perfection of the human capacity to transcend limits by choice.

THE CHOICE TO HIDE

The very antithesis of creative transformation of human limits is, as we have seen, the choice to hide. To the extent that a person strives to understand himself and to value himself, and to share that search with others, there would seem to be no reason for hiding. That we continue to do so, however, is less often the result of a direct choice against the process of maturing in self-knowledge and self-esteem than of a choice in favor of something else.

For one thing, patterns of behavior learned at an early age when we were unable to know any better or discern alternatives tend to persist into adulthood. What parents consistently demand of him spontaneously becomes the guide for the decisions of the child, who has no other norm to refer to. These early habits leave a deep imprint on the child, both because they are the first impressions and because they are allowed to go so long unchallenged. During periods of adolescent rebelliousness he may react against them, but only rarely succeeds in rooting them out. Only when a person has learned to experience feelings as his own, and to share them, in situations where the fear of parental rejection, retaliation, or sanction is not present, can these patterns effectively be changed. Part of this process is learning to accept the fact that the denial of feelings is more counterproductive than the refusal to channel them along paths not of his own choosing.

For another thing, the fear of betrayal encourages the choice to hide from the truth. If parents teach a child that all his needs will be taken care of if he conforms to their wishes, they do him a serious disservice. For the fact is that no human being is capable of satisfying all the needs of any other, and the lie will soon become apparent to the child. If the child could accept it as a lie, he could break free of its control. But children lack the critical faculties for sorting

17

out truth from falsehood in all but very few cases. And since they prefer a dependable world to one filled with distortions at every turn, it is likely that the betrayal will be ignored and the lie twisted into an apparent truth. If the child continues in this pattern, he may never take more than a minimal responsibility for the experiences of his adult life, so preoccupied will he be with placating his superiors and maintaining his dependence on them. Underneath it all he will be seething with anger—against himself for failing to take hold of his life, and against his superiors for tolerating his submissiveness. But at the same time he will be crippled with fear that he would be abandoned if he faced his anger. His fear and anger are dangerous to him and so are hidden, marking the abdication of the very responsibility which would help him. The feeling that does escape is likely only to feed his impotence. He may become a chronic complainer who feels mistreated by the world, or he may tyrannize his household. In any event, his responses will have the cumulative effect of further closing off the paths to self-knowledge and self-esteem.

FORMS OF HIDING

One of the clearest ways to discern the feelings one is hiding is to consider what one most regularly attacks, unfairly, in others, and the forms which those attacks take.

The person who attacks by ridicule communicates his feeling that no one is really good enough for him. His humor is gauged to hurt. His words are barbed and practical jokes humiliating. The rage he wants to deny within himself is visited on others who come near him—friends, acquaintances, and enemies indiscriminately. I remember in high school watching one fellow pull a chair from under a classmate who was about to sit down. The boy fell backwards, lost his balance, and cracked his spine against the

18

chair. He never walked again. The only reaction the prankster could register was one of glassy-eyed surprise: "But I was only kidding." We have all met such practical jokers—although their humor does not often backfire as seriously as it did in the above case—and we can all recognize intuitively the anger hidden behind their pranks. They are not "only kidding," but perhaps kidding only themselves. An angry person who knows he is angry is less a danger to himself and to others than one who denies his anger. And if the anger is held in check by fear, the danger is greater still that it will erupt in damaging and irresponsible ways.

Humor is only one of many possible shelters for hidden feeling. Sexual activity, alcohol, drugs, sleep addiction, athletics, and even schooling can perform the same function. Indeed, any programmed activity can become a ritualized choice of shutting down emotions. The solution, of course, is not to attempt to live without habits, but rather to ensure that our habits reflect our basic values and do not reduce our responsibility towards limit-experiences to reflex reactions.

One of the most subtle forms of hiding is the development of physical symptoms. The body becomes a kind of graveyard of forgotten feelings which do not rest in peace but haunt us with a variety of psychosomatic ailments. Disorders such as high blood pressure, headaches, hemorrhoids, allergies, frigidity, stuttering, constipation, and muscular stiffness can all be signs of troublesome emotions breaking through bodily defenses on the weakest front. These symptoms may in turn trigger more serious disease that might otherwise be avoided.

The idea that physical disorders can be related to the choice to hide feelings should not strike us as terribly odd. Like spontaneous facial and hand movements, posture, blushing, and other nervous signals, these symptoms are a kind of gesture-language for the things we have not yet learned to talk about or otherwise handle in imagination.

What is harder to understand is how an individual can come to prefer reactionary symptomatic illness to the responsibility of facing hidden feelings. At first, the symptoms may be easier to deal with than one's general emotional condition, and so are a welcome alternative. But in time their control increases, imperceptibly but relentlessly. Once a dependence upon symptoms has been set up—for whatever purpose—it can only get stronger and more self-alienating.

As a psychologist, I see my share of "professional cripples," people who waste their time, their energies, and their money rushing about from doctor to doctor, from hospital to hospital, submitting their bodies to every sort of unnecessary surgical mutilation imaginable, literally destroying themselves bit by bit for reasons they cannot explain to themselves, their physicians, or their families. And the final touch comes when they earn the reputation of saint and martyr for their long suffering—when all along they know within themselves that theirs is really a cowardly form of suicide that has simply gotten out of hand.

Closely related to the escape from feelings through physical symptoms is the attempted surrender of one's life to the service of another's happiness. An example may help to describe the effects of such self-imposed slavery.

I knew a woman—let us call her Lillian—whom circumstances had "forced" to remain single her entire life to take care of her mother. When I was a small child I first began visiting her and continued to do so for many years. She constantly talked of all the opportunities in life she had missed because of her loving concern for her mother, and often fantasized about how free she would feel when her mother no longer needed her care. She lived with her mother in a three-bedroom house, but they slept together in the same bed. Her mother died at eighty-five. Lillian immediately fell into a severe depression which lasted two years, and at the end of that time she herself died. Although others could sense her anger at being so dependent on her mother, she insisted to the end that she had had no choice. Had Lillian allowed her feelings some creative, responsible outlet, her life could have been very different. Instead, she chose to live under the illusion that her mother needed her, while it was more true that it was she who needed her mother, even though Lillian was over sixty when her mother died. Her own personal life was unfulfilled because she refused to face the painful realization that serving her mother's needs could never make either of them very happy, and because her mother refused to let go of her little girl long enough for her to become a woman.

GUILT FEELINGS

Let us pause at this point to take up a distinction alluded to earlier between *guilt* and *guilt feelings*. We said there that guilt feelings can be used as a defense against the guilt itself. This is so because guilt is a *rational condition*, whereas guilt feelings represent an *irrational emotional response*. The distinction is important, since the two are frequently confused, and deserves some closer attention.

As a rational condition, guilt is a judgment that some standard of moral behavior has been transgressed. It means simply that a rule or directive which ought to have been followed has been broken. The judgment of guilt says nothing about the reasonableness of the imperative itself. It can apply to civil, ecclesiastical, parental, and philosophical frames of reference, or to any combination of them. The imperative can be just or oppressive. Moreover, the attribution of guilt by itself says nothing about the sanction or punishment appropriate to the transgression. All that is necessary to establish the condition of guilt is that the offended standard be accepted as applicable to the subject in question. This is not to say that the specific norms conditioning a judgment of guilt are unimportant or irrelevant to the process of maturity. Indeed, part of accepting and creatively transforming the experience of guilt as a human limit consists in regular examination and revision of the moral standards which one adopts as part of one's system of values.

Guilt feelings, on the other hand, refer to the class of emotions whose distinguishing characteristic is that they refer to *some* judgment of guilt, which may or may not be appropriate to the behavior in question. They make up the so-called guilty conscience which includes such things as shame, embarrassment, fear of punishment or disapproval, anger, remorse and regret. Since these feelings do not depend on *ad hoc* rational judgments for their appearance in each instance, it is quite possible that they can be provoked by the memory of former judgments no longer held as valid. By the same token, *ad hoc* judgments of guilt can fail to provide us with the accompanying feelings of guilt. We can feel guilty and not be guilty, even as we can be guilty and not feel so. Understanding guilt feelings, therefore, requires insight into the particular rational judgments to which they are attached. Of themselves, feelings of guilt are not adequate guides for reasonable moral decisions. To give them that function would be to exchange the responsibility of behaving in accordance with one's values for relief from the discomfort of the sting of conscience.

Irrational guilt feelings are helpful, then, insofar as they inform us of what our moral judgments at any one moment actually are. They are harmful insofar as they provide us with a place to hide from moral reflection or moral behavior. In this regard, the residue of guilt feelings left by childhood associations with parental injunctions is particularly inimical to adult moral responsibility. Having once

22

been taught that God would punish certain actions or that Santa Claus would pass us by, the emotional reactions which those actions evoke stubbornly survive continued shifts of ethical perspective. That such superstitions outlive their functions ought to be enough to remind us that we can not achieve absolute peace of soul by repressing the creative power of the imagination, denying our limits, and returning to the irresponsible dependencies of childhood.

TRANSFORMING LIMITS

The following verbatim excerpt from a self-determination therapy session illustrates how a man and his sixteen-year-old stepson dealt with a complex limit-situation. The stepfather harbored guilt feelings from a previous marriage which were contributing to a similar failure in his second marriage. The boy's mother was blocking his relationship to his new father, even as father and son were trying to communicate with each other. Altogether, it summarizes much of what this chapter has been saying about pain, failure, frustration, and guilt.

Therapist (to the stepson): I wish you would get beyond your own immediate needs and ask yourself where your life is going in the future, take a good look at your options, and make some better choices.
Stepfather: Look, son, a lot of times in the past I haven't said things to you about what's been happening at home between your mother and me. I never knew really for sure why. I think it was because I didn't trust what you would do with that information. I didn't know how you would handle it. I don't know if it was as much not trusting your ability to handle it as my ability to control the outcome. It was probably a bit of both. But there are going to be a lot of things happening in

the next year and there are a lot of decisions going to be made. I can't make them for you, so I guess you deserve pretty much to know where everything is at.

I talked to your mother last night on the phone. She threw everything at me. Either I dump you and go back or I don't go back at all. (His wife had requested that he not remain on the therapy session with his stepson.) The ultimatum last night was: "If you go there this morning, don't ever come back to this house again." My biggest fear is that you will end up hating her because of the things she says and does. She's a terrified person. She's acting out of fear, like you do a lot. But I don't want you acting like that. I want you to understand. I want you to consider what's happening, to look at how it's affecting your life, and to make your decisions on *that*—not just react the way she does. She's not going to make a session. She's not going to do anything. . . .

Look, I don't know what's going to happen. I don't know how long I'm going to be able to stay there. She said if I leave and try to take you with me, she'll get you back. She'll go to court. She'll do whatever she has to, to keep you from ending up with somebody like me because I'm such a terrible person. Now if that happens, there's not much I can do. It really frightens me to think of the situation it's throwing you into. I don't know what you want me to do. I don't know what you want for yourself. I just don't know where *I* am sometimes. I don't know if you can understand that. She takes every little thing that you do—the shoplifting, the pot—and uses it as another wedge to prove to me what a waste this therapy is. Nothing is working out. I think we've got a lot of bad things between us that we have never gotten out.

24

I don't know how you feel, where you're at or where you're going to. And I want to know.

Stepson: I don't want to stay where she's at. She'll get on my back all the time.

Stepfather: It won't be easy. As Don said, you've got some decisions to make. He's not kidding you. He's giving you straight facts. It's not going to be pleasant, and it's not just you I'm thinking of. I can't hold you up. I can't drag you. If this fight gets to where it looks like it's going, I can't drag you all around. I've enough just trying to keep myself standing up. I've still got a lot of guilt lying back there that she keeps pushing forward and it's not easy to get out from under it. It's not easy for me to see somebody doing what she's doing to herself without feeling like I caused it. I need your help. I want you to be a man for yourself now, all by yourself.

Stepson (Crying): I'm scared.

Stepfather: So am I. I've got to know what's going on. I've got to know when something's wrong. I can't take your shutting down. My biggest fear is that you will end up hating her. I don't know why, but that's all I see now.

Stepson: I don't understand.

Stepfather: I don't either, but I'm just so afraid that you're going to turn against her. I don't want it to be a battle with you and me and her, you and me on one side . . . (Pause) Yeah, I do know why. I'm not your real father. (Pause) As hard as I've tried to be, I'm not. I know how it feels to lose a kid and see him turn away from you. I don't want that to happen to you. I don't want that for her. (Pause) I don't want that for anybody.

Stepson: What am I going to do with her?

Stepfather: What are you going to do with *you*? Stand

25

up! Stand up and show you're a man. You don't have to light up every night, and you don't have to steal booze, and you don't have to go out and shoplift, and you don't have to get involved sexually. You can stand up and do what she expects a man to do. It might make a difference. I don't think it's going to mean she's going to be all right, or it's going to mean everything's different. But you'll be you. You don't have to change her. I've tried. She doesn't want it straight. She wants the power and the control and the conniving games we've been playing for ten years. She wants to be pushed around, she wants to be made to feel like nothing, she wants to keep playing the games. Look, do you really want to leave home, no matter what happens?
Stepson: Yeah.
Stepfather: I don't know what to tell you. I don't have all the answers. I don't even know all the questions. There's something that's been bothering me for a long time though. I've never heard you say anything about it—I mean putting the adoption through. I never knew how you felt about that.
Stepson: I always thought you did your best. I always thought of you as my father. I accepted you as my father.
Stepfather: I never gave you my name.
Stepson: What's a name? You showed me your love but I just turned away from you. (Begins to cry)
Stepfather: We turned away from each other. I was so caught up in my own world for so long I couldn't let anybody in. I'm sorry for that. I can't make up for that, but I can open up to you now. I want you to know why I never went through with the adoption. I would never admit it to myself before. I couldn't take the guilt for

26

walking out on my family (previous marriage). I couldn't totally accept you as my son, as hard as I tried. There was too much guilt there. It just kept getting in the way. I couldn't give you everything. I could be your father in a material way. I could *be* there. But I couldn't give you my name. I thought you hated me for that. I wanted to go through with it and get it done.

Stepson: The way you talked, I always thought that it was impossible.

Stepfather: Just about. I tried and tried to get him (the boy's father) to sign the papers. I went to an attorney a couple of years ago again, and he said if I file it might be six months or a year. And he did nothing on it, and I never did any more about it. All those wasted years. I don't want to waste any more. (Pause) It's not easy to do anything when you don't know the outcome, but you're going to grow up. Nobody's going to stop you. I really believe you can do just about anything you want to.

Stepson: I just can't believe it.

Stepfather: We can't repair the past. I've turned my back on you in the past and I don't want you to shut down on me again—no matter what happens. Don't let anybody put you down. You're worth standing up for.

At this point the father stood up and embraced his son—something they had both wanted to do for years. There was still the pain of not being able to share their feelings with the mother and wife. But in their affection there was great courage.

There is no instant cure for dealing with feelings too long hidden. The process is slow and tedious—and certainly more painful than leaving them alone. And even when they are brought to light, the increased responsibility can be discomforting in the extreme. The stepfather in our example understood this, and through him his stepson was beginning to understand. But unless we are willing to take that first courageous step in the face of our limits, the possibility of creative, transforming choice can never be ours.

CHAPTER THREE

BEGINNINGS

It was Sigmund Freud's view that, being born into a sick and twisted world, we must all become a bit sick and twisted ourselves. There is no denying Freud's appreciation of man's inhumanity to man, and his insight into its institutionalization in cultural forms. Where I part paths with him is in his conclusion that our best response is to civilize our discontents by tailoring our values and behavior to the world about us. I prefer to view mature responsibility more in terms of corrective choices stemming from a deliberated dis-ease with all forms of inhumanity, personal and social.

Man is distinct from the animal in his ability to order and control his future; but he is also free to refuse this privilege. To one degree or another, he can surrender his powers of self-determination in favor of adjusting to the demands of immediate needs, external conditions, or the expectations of others. It is this failure of self-determination that is, in my opinion, at the bottom of all misunderstanding of emotional pathology. We get sidetracked if we limit the treatment of such disorders simply to the relief of pain. More central is an insight into the existential discord that results from man's ability to imagine and to desire what he cannot in fact attain. Refusal to accept and deal with this dilemma of limits discussed in the last chapter is, I am convinced, the ultimate source of all forms of irresponsible behavior, including the failure to seek a human meaning to patterns of behavior established in childhood.

FEELINGS FROM THE PAST

Already in infancy we experience some sense of our inability to satisfy our own needs by virtue of our instinctual dependence on those about us who inevitably prove undependable on occasion. If the shock of awareness comes too strong too soon, the effects can be traumatic for later life. In like manner, as we grow older, we also learn of our inability to satisfy our parents' needs, and here too the impact of the child's experience of failure can have devastating consequences for his emotional responses as an adult.

Overcoming these and similar traumata of our early years begins with truthfulness—accepting them as part of our experience—but must not stop there. Valuing our capacity for self-determination requires that we do not accept their conditioning effects as irreversible, but seek to correct them by the choices we make for the future. And these choices in turn find their confirmation and support in the care we experience from others and show them in return.

Unfortunately, we too often distort the function of self-determination by directing our efforts to correcting the past, which only increases its control over us. To recapitulate in present relationships the dissatisfactions of past relationships with one's parents or other significant individuals, in the hopes of mending memories, is only self-defeating. To expect others to do what our parents did not, and perhaps could not do, is unfair to ourselves, to those on whom we make the demands, and even to our parents. In this regard, I remember well the advice which the mother of one of my patients, a twenty-year-old man, gave her son: "Your father and I raised you with mistakes. Our parents

30

raised us the same way. And unless *you* change, you will do the same thing with your children and they will end up complaining about you instead of changing their own lives."

THE LESSONS OF RESTRAINT

In many and subtle ways, modern western culture teaches parents to place excessive importance on the image their children have of them. To this end they hide their faults, their pains, and their mistakes from their children as far as possible. And the children respond by helping to protect the fragile image of perfection which their parents value above all else. Respect thus comes to be identified in the child's mind with simple obedience. "Honor thy father and thy mother" is interpreted as "Don't upset thy father and thy mother." As long as the child needs parental approval to survive and fears abandonment or rejection, he learns not to challenge inconsistencies and imperfections. In short, he learns to restrain and hide his feelings, instead of learning to translate them into rational terms and evaluate them more objectively. He plays dumb, since admitting that he understands his situation would be too dangerous. Or else he makes every effort to justify his parents' actions and words, since admitting that they were unfair or incorrect would be too great a responsibility for his inexperience.

In the same way the child comes to accept and to protect the image which his parents give him of himself. If the child is accused of being a "bad boy," he will try to be "good" if he thinks being "bad" threatens the image of his parents as rational authorities. But if the accusation is interpreted as his parents' image of him, he may just as well continue to be bad in order to confirm the supremacy of their judgment. In either case the fundamental lesson is the same: personal

31

feelings must be channeled along the lines of the parental expectations.

The lessons of restraint, if taught forcefully enough and early enough, can continue to form adult patterns of behavior as long as one neglects to assume the responsibility for them. I remember seeing a missionary once who had been stationed in Asia for a number of years. In the eyes of his church superiors, he had been successful and productive. He had built a school, a church, and a clinic, and had managed to integrate his Western religious ideals in a foreign and often unreceptive culture. Proud of what he had done to bring "truth" to the "heathen," he was back on home leave. Departing his mother's house early one evening, he was told: "Now you be sure to be in by 10:30." "Mother, I'm a grown man," he replied. "I'm over fifty years old. I can take care of myself quite well enough and decide what time to come in." He stayed out until 2:30 in the morning and arrived back at the house drunk and depressed. When I asked him what time he had started drinking, he said, "About 10:30 or 11:00—why? What has that got to do with it?" Unwittingly he had proved correct his mother's image of him: that he was still too little to be out so late.

The child strives to please his parents to earn their acceptance, and avoids displeasing them so as not to be rejected. As we have seen, this often entails denying expression to his own emotions as they surface. If parents do not want their child frightened, he learns how to suppress fear. If they disapprove of the child's becoming angry, he learns to bridle his anger. If affection is tolerated only at certain times and within certain limits, the child learns to restrain himself accordingly. Like young animals in the wild, children are masters of the art of survival in the jungle of psychological relationships that surround them. Not only do they protect their dependencies on their parents, but they manage to postpone outlawed emotions and secure their expression in substitute forms under safer conditions. But here again, whether the displacement is successful or not is secondary. The fact that substitution has been adopted as a means of adjustment to a threatening situation is enough to establish a pattern that can only prove an impediment to later emotional maturity.

BREAKING PATTERNS

If childhood patterns based on the belief that expressing emotions endangers parental love and attention are long allowed to go unexamined, it becomes increasingly difficult for adult relationships to form without severe interference from the past. The individual may seek affection, for instance, by guarding his own emotions. Or he may systematically force those who try to get close to him into parental roles. In both cases he effectively destroys the thing he most wants. Similarly, if a person was afraid of his mother as a child, he may protect that pattern of relationship by extending it to all women. The more he tries to approach women, the more apt he then is to distance himself by shyness, panic, anger, or domination. Alternatively, he may avoid women altogether to ensure that they do not provoke the pain and fear he experienced as a child.

Breaking free of our beginnings without denying them is difficult, but not impossible. One of the most impressive examples I know involved a patient of mine who was raised in a semiprimitive tribe. His father was chief of the tribe, which meant that his authority was above question. He was the law. The patient, when he was six years old, lost a key, which turned out to be a very important key, though the boy did not realize it. When his father discovered the fact, he went into a rage and beat the child brutally, dislocating his jaw. He then stripped the boy naked and sent him out of the house for a week's punishment. The rest of the tribe was ordered not to offer the boy medical attention, food, clothing, or shelter under penalty of severe retaliation from the chief. This small child was forced to live without attention, unfed, unclothed, uncared for, and unsheltered for seven days, abandoned by everyone—because he lost a key. In over twenty years of practice, I have never heard a more horrifying story. The experience ought, perhaps, to have traumatized the boy severely for life. But it did not. When I met him, he was a young man in his twenties, studying to be a Christian missionary. This is what he told me: "I knew my father was wrong in doing that to me. I knew he shouldn't have treated me that way. I also knew I couldn't do anything about it at the time. I was hurt. I was angry and I was very, very frightened. But I knew he was wrong to treat me that way and I knew that he shouldn't have done it. A long time later I talked to my father about it. He told me he too knew he had done wrong, but that he was afraid to ask my forgiveness. I told him I could not forget what had happened, but that I had long since forgiven him."

By choosing to accept the difference between his father's behavior and his own worth, this young man had freed himself from the possible devastating control his past might have wrought on his future. He did not need to live the rest of his life terrified of displeasing those placed in authority over him or attempting to retaliate against the injustice and the pain he had suffered as a child. He chose to become a missionary, returning to his tribe, as he put it, "to teach them that love and care are a better way to treat one another than fear and violence." Had he refused to face his feelings, he would likely be a very disturbed individual today. Without the aid of professional psychotherapy, he had somehow managed to sort out the knotted tangle of emotions which for years had left him scarred, confused, and withdrawn. When he talked about his experience, it was with a great deal of feeling. He wept and snarled and trembled as he told his story, but he was at peace with both his emotions and his intellectual judgments. He had learned creatively to accept the responsibility for what someone else had done to him.

THE ROOTS OF PRETENSE

Feelings of themselves are spontaneous, nonrational, and never moral or immoral. When we assign moral values to a feeling, we are either confusing the emotion with its particular form of expression, or else simply not understanding what the feeling is. Yet moralizing feelings is precisely what accounts for that repression or displacement which denies them their rightful function in our lives. Categorizing feelings themselves as good or evil, establishing circumstances in which they "ought" or "ought not" to show up, is, in the first place, ineffective. Feelings remain forever indifferent to the labels we put on them and oblivious to the laws we set up for their propriety. More important, though, the moral classification of an emotion is a counterproductive way of exercising choice over how we shall express it. Moralizing a feeling rather than its various forms of expression means ignoring responsibility in favor of simple reflex reaction—whether by allowing the feeling immediate and uncritical expression, or by repressing it and thereby handing it over to the unconscious processes of displacement.

The various ways we devise to hide from our feelings were treated in the previous chapter. Our particular concern here is the way that the child learns to distrust what he feels, and to pattern that distrust in his behavior.

Young animals in their natural habitats do not become emotionally disturbed the way young humans do, because their emotions are not inhibited from immediate expression by "well-intentioned" parents. As a result, the animal does not need to hide its feelings, whereas the child may often be forced to revert to pretense to cover up emotions whose expression he judges unsafe.

Children do not have to be taught *how* to pretend; it is natural to their powers of imagination. But they can be taught *what* to pretend, and *when*. Parental example and communication—verbal or nonverbal—can lead a child to extend his "make-believe" world to making his parents believe he is feeling one thing when in fact he is feeling another. There is no doubt that children are themselves surprisingly perceptive in locating pretense in adults. But that very ability, which could be used to help teach them honesty with their emotions, is often itself forced into hiding. An example may help.

I remember when I was going to college and trying to pay my way through school by conducting door-to-door interviews for an opinion research center. It was a cardinal rule that we could not begin an interview after 9:00 p.m.; how long it continued after that was unimportant. I was paid a fixed amount for each questionnaire I returned, and so naturally tried to arrange my schedule so as to complete as many as possible before the deadline. One particular evening, around 8:00 p.m., I was interviewing a woman whose household duties were making the interview next to impossible. Between answering the telephone and taking care of her children, the ten-minute interview was taking her forever. Her four year-old son kept demanding attention; and, hoping to save time, I placed him on my lap, gave him some candy, bounced him up and down, and even read him a story during one of the telephone calls. All the while I was growing more and more anxious as the minutes ticked away. When we finally finished, it was already past 9:00 p.m. I thanked the woman politely and began to leave. The four-year-old boy stood in my path, looked straight up at me, and blurted out, "Why don't you like me?". I was speechless. He was right, of course, but I had not expected him to see through my pleasant manners. His mother was upset by the question and reminded him that I had given him candy, held him on my lap and read him a story, and that he was a bad boy for talking to me like that. At the time I was grateful for her saving me from embarrassment. Only later did I realize how much better it would have been had she accepted his question about my pretense and taken the occasion to teach him a lesson about how we hurt others when we hide what we feel from them.

Acknowledging a feeling, as I have said, enables us to choose, from among a variety of alternatives, that expression which seems most appropriate to the state of feeling and the circumstances in which it appeared. It may even lead to the choice not to express in the immediate context; but this is different from contrived expression, whose main function is to deny the feeling to others by *denying it to ourselves*.

Fear and anger are the clearest examples of how this process can be programmed in the child, since their expressive forms tend to be so out of character with the lessons of parlor etiquette which preoccupy so much of the typical parents' time in educating their children. Less obvious, but no less effective, are the lessons we are taught as children about dealing with affection. If mother and father are vying with each other for the child's affection, the child is made a pawn in a game, with the impossible task of making both sides win. He learns that what he feels spontaneously can be threatening to one or the other parent, and so has little choice but to pretend affection where he does not feel it, or pretend indifference where he feels affectionate. Unless a child so conditioned can later reverse these patterns of behavior, it is all too likely he will end up repeating them in his adult relationships. Worse still, he may teach them to his own children, demanding of them a spontaneous affection he has never been able to trust in himself and so forcing them into the same patterns that govern his own life.

BEGINNING AGAIN

To value the power of self-determination is to believe in the capacity of the human to begin again, to correct by choice the habits of estrangement he has learned as a child, and to prevent their contagion from spreading to his children. The following taped verbatim excerpt, taken from a group I am working with even as I write these pages, dramatizes this capacity. It has to do with a middle-aged woman who had a daughter out of wedlock and a son by a marriage which had ended in divorce, and who was living with her two children in a common-law marriage.

Valerie: I'm worried about Laura (her daughter). She's insisted on getting a boy's haircut and has even taken a boy's name.
Therapist: And she's how old?
Valerie: Nine and a half. I know what's going on, I think. She's jealous of Tad (her brother and Valerie's son). She thinks she'll get more attention and approval from me by being a boy. The problem is, I think she's right, since I told her one of the reasons that I didn't like her is that she is a girl.
Therapist: No wonder she's trying to change.
Valerie: Yeah, I know. Okay, I guess—I mean, I know—I'm not facing something. It's just that I'm afraid of the things I don't like about Laura, like that she doesn't have the same last name as Tad and I . . . It's all such a mess. I feel so alone. (Valerie began to weep softly here, try as she might to stifle her tears, and became more withdrawn and quiet so that her words

were barely audible. She was clearly afraid of what she had to say and what she might feel about it.)

Therapist: That hits you, doesn't it? That really hits you. Stop right there. What exactly does that do to you?

Valerie: I think she's lonely, too. I think she's picked up on the idea that she's the one that doesn't *belong*, and that if she changed her sex somehow she would.

Therapist: I think you've got pretty good *insight* into it.

Valerie: Yeah, but that's not enough. It doesn't make it any better or change anything.

Therapist: What I meant was, maybe there's something else going on. You know, if she were a boy, how apt would she be to go and get herself pregnant? Might you not be protecting her from your own kind of mistake?

Valerie: I don't know.

Therapist: You know, one way to look at this is that you might be trying to show real concern underneath all your attacks.

Valerie: Oh yeah, because when this was brought to my attention, the one thing that went through my mind was: okay, Tad is seeing someone who can teach *him* how to be a man. (Tad was seeing a male therapist.)

Therapist: And can *you* really teach *her* how to be a woman?

Elizabeth: Or teach her to be a better woman than you?

Alex: Or is she going to make the same mistakes you made, and end up as unhappy as you?

Therapist: It hasn't gotten that far yet.

Valerie: But it eventually would.

Therapist: Just how afraid *are* you that she might turn out like you?

Valerie: I don't know what you mean by "how afraid." I don't know.

Therapist: Well, one way to protect her from getting

pregnant and having a child out of wedlock would be to teach her to be a boy, and hope she ends up relating sexually only to other women.

Valerie: Okay. (Pause) But I don't see *that* as a good life for her.

Therapist: Which would be better: for her to have the kind of life you've had up to a couple of years ago (when Valerie began in therapy), or to be a lesbian?

Valerie: To be a lesbian.

Therapist: And that's what you're teaching her, in effect. (Pause) That angers me, it really angers me. My sense of it is: who the hell do you think you are that you're that powerful? You're playing God with your daughter's life, making her decisions for her, assuming that she's going to make the same bad choices you did.

Valerie: I didn't realize it.

(I felt strongly about Valerie's manipulation of her daughter, and decided my personal feelings needed expression at that point. Assuming that her child had no choice of her own in determining what kind of life she would lead was simply unfair. In order to help Valerie to release her own feelings, I then made use of Nathaniel Branden's Sentence-Completion Technique. The patient had used the technique before when dealing with her tendency to withdraw from her emotions.)

Therapist: Would you stand up, please and work on this sentence: Whenever I am ready to forgive myself. . .

Valerie: Whenever I am ready to forgive myself . . . (Beginning to tremble)

Therapist: Go on.

Valerie: Whenever I am ready to forgive myself . . . (Begins to cry)

Therapist: Don't stop there.

Valerie: Whenever I am ready to forgive myself
. . . (Valerie is hardly able to say the beginning of the
sentence this time.)

Therapist: Let it go, Valerie.

Valerie (Sobbing uncontrollably): Whenever . . . I'm
ready to . . . forgive myself . . . (Shaking all over and
crying loudly, she can hardly speak.)

Therapist: Come on, Valerie, complete the sentence.

Valerie: Whenever I'm ready to forgive
myself . . . then I won't expect so much from other
people. I won't expect so much from myself. (Breaks
into tears again)

Therapist: It hurts, doesn't it?

(There was no point in coddling the patient to relieve
her pain—quite the contrary. Valerie needed to stop
being protected from what she felt. She remained on
her feet, shaking violently and hardly able to maintain
balance. As she regained equilibrium, I went on.)

Therapist: Just close your eyes and sink into what
you're feeling right now.

Valerie: I'm feeling scared.

Therapist: Work with this sentence now: What I'm beginning to feel is . . .

Valerie: What I'm beginning to feel is fear. What I'm
beginning to feel is loneliness. What I'm beginning to
feel right now is calmer.

Therapist: What I haven't told my daughter might
be . . .

Valerie: What I haven't told my daughter might be
. . . (Pause) . . . that I really *do* care about about
her.

Therapist: Yes, you do.

Valerie: I don't want her to make the same mistakes as I
did.

Therapist: I think it's very important to tell her that.

41

Valerie: I don't know why I haven't.

Therapist: I think you might try.

Valerie: I really *am* afraid that she is going to make the same mistakes that I did and I really *do* care about her, that she doesn't make the same mistakes.

Therapist: Are you willing to talk to her about this and come back next week and let us know what happened? Because a couple of things strike me. One is the excessive demands you place on yourself for doing things you really can't do; and the other thing is the unwillingness to forgive your own past, assuming that the damage has to be permanent. Those are two things I don't think you've told Laura. It is okay to be uncertain.

Valerie: I guess that's the way I try to keep control. Even if I do something wrong, at least I'm doing *something* and don't feel quite so helpless. I almost feel like it was better to do something wrong than not do anything at all, because I felt I'd just be all alone if I didn't do anything, and I couldn't stand that feeling.

Therapist: I'll be interested in hearing your report next week after you've talked to Laura. Give yourself a chance to settle down, though. A couple of days, maybe. Then go and talk to her. Does anyone want to respond?

Alex: I like what you're doing. And I like *you* a lot, too. I don't think I ever told you that. I remember there was a time a couple of years ago, joking around or something like that, that I'd always come out with the line: "Hell, no, I'm never having any kids. What if they turned out like me?" Well, it's been a long time since then. I hope when I do have kids that they won't have to go through what I've been through. But I sure as heck hope they'll do it on their own, whatever they do.

Valerie: Yeah.

Therapist: Do you see the difference there, Valerie?

Valerie: Yeah.

Therapist: Does anyone else want to respond?

Elizabeth: Yeah, I understand that particularly with my own daughters. Like my oldest daughter: I see things in her that I don't like in myself. Reluctance to get close to people, more so than anybody in the house. And it hurts because she got it from me. But I can change and so can she.

(After several others had responded, the session came to a close. A week later Valerie returned to the group. She began with a big smile.)

Valerie: I'd like to report on my "homework." It was a couple of days after I talked about it. I sat down and told Laura I would like to talk to her. One thing I learned—just about children, or just about Laura—is that when I get heady with her it really confuses her. And that's what I was doing. And she was getting confused, and started to cry. And I asked her, "Why are you crying?" She said, "Because I don't know where your head is." I thought that was neat—that she knew that, I mean. So I decided to tell her specifically what I liked and what I didn't like. And I told her that I didn't like the fact that she was dressing up like a boy, that she was calling herself by a boy's name. And I told her that the thing that really bothered me about her was that she wasn't accepting who she was. She wasn't accepting that she was nine-year-old Laura, a girl. And I said that hurt me. And angered me. And I told her about when I was a little girl, how I kept things inside of me, and was a lot like she is. I told her how often I get overwhelmed by the responsibility of having to raise children, without always knowing what to do. And she just kind of sat there and listened. And when I paused, she was getting a kind of screwed-up face and just let it out, starting to cry. She came over to me and I hugged her. She said

43

she had wanted to tell me for two years how really scared she had been. A lot of hurt came out, about home, about school.

Therapist: So where does that leave you?

Valerie: Well, I can see that what I was avoiding with Laura was really what I was feeling about her—and about myself. This thing about being a boy, I think it was that she couldn't relate to other girls because I was getting in the way.

Therapist: Is that all?

Valerie: What do you mean?

Therapist: I mean, I am picking up a gap between what you're saying and how you're saying it. If I had learned so much from a situation, I'd be absolutely delighted.

Valerie: I was. I *was*. (Smiling) And I was anxious to tell you all about it.

Therapist: That's a feeling, too, a pleasant one. And just as important as the unpleasant ones. And not worth hiding.

Parents often complain of a communication gap with their children, when in fact more often than not it is simply that they do not want to accept what their children are communicating to them: a reflection of themselves. Raising children is a special kind of privilege. Repeating the mistakes of the past with one's children is an abuse of that privilege and of the children themselves, who are forced to bear the burden of growing up under the emotional handicaps they have inherited from their parents. At the same time, it will not do to ignore the unwillingness of so many young people to accept the responsibility for their youth. In the last analysis, far more important than apportioning blame is choosing to correct the damage. This and this alone is the reason why psychotherapy is concerned with returning to beginnings.

44

CHAPTER FOUR

IMAGINING

Of all the things we humans are endowed with, surely none is so full of powers and marvels as the ordinary gift of imagination. Its realm is vast enough to gather up the seas and embrace the heavens, and still have room to reach out to the worlds yet unseen. It forges the tools to create a civilization and the tools to destroy it. It is the romping ground for memory of things past and the testing ground for hope of things to come. It gives visions to the young and dreams to the old. It is indeed the very likeness of God stamped on the human soul.

There is no such thing as a person who cannot imagine. Imagination is an inherited biological capacity whose possibilities for development are almost boundless. While the ability to imagine matures with age, however, it is never as free and unrestricted as in childhood. Not knowing enough about how the world is, or understanding enough about how it ought to be, the child plays with the little he does know and understand. He will not, as a rule, *confuse* the real world with the imaginary, but he will often *combine* the two in creating games. In this way, imagination is the child's most reliable defense against the disappointments and limitations he comes to experience as he grows older. It is loyal and obedient. It can be conjured up at will to offer a retreat from frustration or tedium. It may even take the form of a special imaginary friend who supplies whatever things experience denies him. In short, imagining is the child's way of taking his first halting steps in self-determination.

EXPERIMENTING WITH IMAGINING

No matter how many restrictions the accumulated experience of a lifetime place on the use and trust of imagination, it is impossible—save in cases of severe brain damage or other mental retardation—*not* to imagine, given the proper stimulus. "A white horse"—the very words release memory and fantasy uncontrollably, making it impossible to suppress at least some vague picture, however fleeting. Even were I to say, "Do *not* think of a white horse," the negative suggestion is powerless to stop the process. At the same time, such external stimulus to imagination is always and unavoidably partial; internal conditions peculiar to each imagination necessarily accompany it. Even an imagination that is highly disciplined and controlled (whether by myself or by another) devises its own distortions and surfaces spontaneously, blissfully disrespectful of our rules and prohibitions.

As an example, try the following. Imagine for five seconds—a mountain. Given just this simple instruction, your mountain will differ considerably from mine, depending in part on mountains you've seen and on your memory for visual perceptions. And even if you've never actually seen a mountain, some image will have become associated with that word, enabling you to create a fantasy all your own.

Now imagine a mountain made of solid gold . . . with a snow-capped peak . . . and a cactus growing right out of the top . . . and on top of the cactus is a large sign that reads "HELLO" in flashing blue lights . . . with a red border. The mountain is very steep . . . and flat on top . . . with a purple fence around the cactus plant . . . which isn't really

46

a cactus at all, but an evergreen, a blue spruce . . . no, yellow . . . no, striped in yellow, blue and green.

Notice how each suggestion is incorporated into the image almost as quickly as it can be made, and how the image changes as you add or subtract further data. Notice too how pausing to talk about the process makes the image begin to fade. . . . Oops! The mountain has just turned into a little mouse. All of this is possible precisely because images take on a life of their own once freed of dependence on immediate external perceptions.

Now let us try an experiment in imagining muscular activity. First place your palms together firmly and bring your arms together all the way up to the elbows. Then picture a heavy rope being wound tightly about your hands, over your wrists and halfway up your arms, with a thick double knot at each end. Keep your hands and arms together as you focus on the image, giving it a while to register and take shape. Now try to pull your hands apart without changing the image; you will find it extremely difficult, if not altogether impossible, to perform this elementary muscular feat. Try it. And notice how, when your hands finally do come apart, the image is immediately dissolved.

Or, again, imagine yourself tied up as before; but this time tell yourself that at the count of three the rope will turn into a spider's web, easily broken by the slightest movement. Ready? Hands and arms tightly bound? Then here goes—one . . . two . . . three! Your hands come apart easily. If you followed this exercise in your mind, you will have noticed that as your arms moved apart, there was a flashing mental picture of thin, fragile, grey threads waving about.

THE NATURE OF IMAGINING

Such primitive experiments as the above serve to show how imagination can be stimulated to activity by things other than direct perception, and how these "unreal" images can be extremely powerful. Indeed, in certain circumstances (such as dream states and similar states of relative unconsciousness), they can be every bit as powerful and have the same effect as if we had judged ourselves actually present in the conditions depicted imaginatively. That in turn enables us to see how it is the *stimulated activity* of imagining which is felt as real and powerful, not the *source of the stimulus*. Hence, when someone complains of lacking a vivid imagination, unless he has severe sensory disorders he means to say that he is unhappy with being able to imagine vividly except when certain kinds of stimuli are present.

Further, just as imagining is a response to stimuli, so too it can become the stimulus for other nonimaginative responses. In our last example, words stimulated images which in turn stimulated certain muscular reactions. This process may help us better to understand what is meant by talk of controlling the mind or washing the brain. Imagination belongs to the realm of perception, not of rational decision. And, like any perception, it can trigger habitual reflex reactions of a nonrational nature. These can be autonomic or acquired. If acquired, they can be taught by external conditioning or learned through self-discipline. The effect of the lesson is the same: a certain form of activity follows upon a certain form of perception without the need for an intervening rational decision. In this sense, trusting our eyes as reliable guides for moving about, trusting our hands on the keyboard of the typewriter without having to look, and trusting that lunch is ready when mother calls "Come and get it" are all examples of "mind control."

Moral judgment relates to the use of imagination only at those points where rational decision is possible. Habits of response acquired as a result of choice—one's own or another's—are thus open in part to moral examination, whereas those inherited by nature are not. Exactly what one accepts as conditioning essential to social living (e.g., the learning of language) and what one rejects as brainwashing (e.g., the learning of racial prejudice) depends on the horizons of one's particular moral standards. But the actual activity of imagining itself can never be considered either moral or immoral. Under whatever natural or imposed conditions imagination is made to function, and to whatever purpose it is directed, *as imagination* it is as spontaneous and amoral as feeling emotions or perceiving objects. The products of imagination are never "good" or "bad" of themselves; they simply *are*.

FEAR OF IMAGINING

The most unnatural and destructive form of mind control is the attempt to teach another to be afraid of what he might imagine. In one way or another, this sin against human nature always involves the error of moralizing imagination. Frequently it also involves a certain cultural and historical myopia which seeks to protect its own interests by condemning whatever looks beyond the conventional limits of the good and true. Yet the tyranny of reason over imagination is not illogical. It argues that since illicit and sinful behavior is a result of rational decisions generated and planned in fantasy, it makes good sense to disinfect the processes of imagination before they can lead to destructive behavior. The problem with such an approach, of course, is that it esteems living by adjustment to what is proper over living by choice.

Consider religious prohibitions against "bad thoughts," i.e., against imagining activities which, if decided upon as a course of action, would be immoral according to the ethical norms which set up the prohibition. Fortunately, attempts so to launder the products of imagination are only rarely wholly successful. Try as we might to shut down an image and deny it, it is nearly impossible to do so completely. To the extent that we can repress the image, we may be rid of it temporarily; but imagination is not so easily overcome. In moments when our critical faculties are lowered, the fantasy returns to catch us off guard. Were this not the case, automatizing ourselves would be a relatively simple task. Unfortunately, failure to repress the fantasy is often accompanied by feelings of guilt, which only further lower self-esteem and increase the desire for self-automation. Worse still, this may lead in turn to symptomatic, though morally irreprehensible, forms of behavior. Much obsessive-compulsive activity falls into this category, including the escape into religious ritualism. We end up in nonproductive activities without knowing why, closing the circle which began with the "bad thoughts" without ever having to criticize the reasonableness of the original prohibition.

We most generally flee imagination because we fear the consequences of what we might imagine. Many of us would be jailed or locked up in a mental asylum if ten minutes of our imaginative productions were translated into behavior. Actually, when we refuse to accept our imaginings as our own, we are *more* apt, not less, to end up in jails or asylums. An enemy who can *imagine* giving me a pounding, and yet chooses not to *do* so, is not so dangerous to me as one who "couldn't imagine ever getting violent with me." The latter is so afraid of hurting me, and the consequences of doing so, that he denies the image rather than freely decide not to act it out. But disowning an image, disallowing its possibility, restricts his choice and therefore harms him more than it protects either of us.

I remember vividly one man participating in a group therapy session that ran several days. He was getting more

50

and more furious with me as time went on, but kept insisting I need not be afraid because the thought of attacking someone in anger seemed "ridiculous" to him. He had no reason to hurt me, he said, but his denials seemed only to make his facial muscles more taut, his body more tense, his voice more strained. My foot was in a cast at the time as a result of an injury incurred some months previously. I told the man that I feared his attack and hoped he would find some way of expressing his feelings fully, whatever they were, without doing me physical violence. The next morning the cast was removed. I was back in the room with the group less than five minutes when he jumped at me, grabbed the injured foot, and twisted it viciously. There was no mistaking that he had grabbed for my weakest point. His reply to me, in my pain, was simply: "I don't know what came over me. I didn't know what I was doing." It would have been better for both of us if he could have admitted that in fact he was angry enough to strike out at me and *then* decided not to.

THE CHOICE TO IMAGINE

Sad to say, many people who suffer from repressions of imagination are often treated in ways that reaffirm their problem, when they should be offered afresh and without intimidation the choice to imagine.

The depressed individual who wallows in his helplessness for fear of failure is often merely waited on out of pity. The phobic is told not to worry, or is shielded from what he fears, rather than encouraged to make use of his imagination in order to seek out the real object of his displaced fear. Moreover, I am convinced that a great deal of psychophysical maladjustment and emotional disturbance now entrusted to medication, religiosity, and schooling could

51

with more profit be turned over to the nonaddictive healing power of imagining.

The choice to hide and the forms of hiding described earlier affect imagining every bit as much as they affect feeling. They isolate one further and further from the truth and intimacy of one's life. Insight alone is not enough to reverse this process. Feeling and fantasy must be liberated by choice, and trusted once again as integral parts of being fully alive to one's self and others. The special importance of imagining here is that it forms a link between emotions and understanding. By allowing feelings to be dramatized in images, one can gain an insight into them that is otherwise inaccessible; and by allowing judgments an imaginative expression, their feeling-tones can be recaptured.

A frequent side effect of the choice to imagine without one's customary restraints is a recovery of the fullness of language. It is always fascinating to see the way in which the artificial dialects serving parlor etiquette, higher education, thick-skinned vulgarity, or any other social role one has cast oneself in collapse under the weight of everything loosed in free imagining. The mother superior of a convent begins to swear like a truck-driver; the learned professor babbles on like a little child; the tough motorcycle cop turns to the romantic tenderness of birthday-card poetry. One patient of mine, a woman, put it beautifully after an unexpected outburst of crudity: "I never even thought I *knew* those words, let alone was able to *use* them. But I couldn't think of any other way of saying what it was I felt." The restriction and emancipation of language reminds us once again that just as our choice to hide divides and isolates, so does our choice to imagine reunite us in a bond of deep and common humanity.

THERAPEUTIC IMAGINING

A study of the great variety of techniques developed over the past century of psychological science for working therapeutically with imagination would of itself be sufficient tribute to the miracle of imagination. More significantly, together they represent perhaps the single most impressive demonstration of a fact essential to any sound psychotherapy: that, in the end, it is the patient who heals himself, or no healing takes place.

In the verbatim excerpt which follows, Henry is a twenty-nine-year-old social worker with a history of grandiose idealism coupled with inefficient planning and little action. He had been on the brink of severe emotional breakdown several times, and entered therapy in order to attempt to reorganize his life more effectively.

Henry: Do you remember the supervisor at work I told you about? Well, another thing happened today. I came in and we were going to discuss the details of a program. I started to talk to her and her co-worker about it, and it was like they had everything mapped out and planned the way they wanted to do it. And I found myself just fighting this, you know. "How dare you plan without consulting me or without letting me in on it . . ." But now I don't know. That was kind of unfair, because she does . . . she does handle that side of it, and I'm thinking now . . . I don't know, I was fighting here and not realizing why.

Therapist: What?

Henry: Everything I would say, she would pull out a piece of paper or say "Well, here is what was decided on last week. This is what the program is all about, you know."

Therapist: I'd like to get more of a picture of what's going on between you and this woman. Is there anyone

53

who thinks he can role-play Henry? I'd like to see Henry play the boss and have someone else play Henry.

Mike: I'll do it.

Therapist (to Henry): I would like you first of all to set the scene, so as to give Mike some idea of how he's supposed to handle it.

Henry: Okay. (to Mike) You come in. You've got some program plans that you've brought in and you've arranged this time to talk to the boss about it. So you just get into what I've just been trying to say now, when you play me. You have a report that has to get done for the agency. There are about four sections to it. You've done these reports a lot of times, so you're good at it, you know.

Therapist (to Mike): Do you have it?

Mike: I think so. Let's try.

Henry (playing his boss): Would you put that stuff down over there?

Mike: Well, I have something to talk about. I have these reports to get in. I know I've done them in the past, but I'd just like you to check.

Henry: Oh, fine, Henry, fine. You want to get our ideas on the clients, is that it? (To therapist) Wait a minute, where's the co-worker?

Mike: I have this one idea, about having this room painted yellow.

Therapist (to Henry, who looks puzzled): Just carry on with your role, and let Mike play you as he wants.

Henry: Okay . . . Painted *yellow*?

Mike: Yeah, the paint's chipping and it's, you know . . .

Henry: You're going to paint . . .

Mike: So if we had it painted yellow, with maybe some little designs on it or something . . .

Henry: Well, I've heard from the agency, and they

don't want any yellow rooms. They'd rather have them blue.

Mike: Okay, blue. Just some brighter color, you know. And the second thing was to get better chairs. The chairs are . . . I mean, the seats are falling off of them. One kid got cut on them.

Henry: I think that's a great idea. Where are we going to get them?

Mike: I don't know. There are a lot of places that make school chairs. It shouldn't cost more than fifty dollars to get them fixed.

Henry: That's a good idea.

Mike: And the third thing, a better microphone system, because when you're in the auditorium you need to . . . the people aren't hearing you, and you need to . . .

Henry: Hold on, here is the program plan. Our microphone system is going to have two in front and two in back.

Mike: It was just an idea. Well, okay.

Henry (giving instructions to Mike on how to play his role): Now you just get up and walk away.

Therapist: Hold it there. Don't program him. I just asked you to feed into what he is saying, whatever it is, and respond to him. Look at how you're trying to program him. (Henry was doing little more than trying to remember specific scenes, and was acting without emotions. He looked more "on stage" than "into the role." I decided to turn to another technique, in order to focus on Henry's need to control the role-playing situation: the Sentence-Completion Technique shown in the last chapter.)

Therapist: I want you to try to finish this sentence with the first answers that occur to you. And look at Mike. But stop the role-playing. Be yourself again. Okay?

Henry: Okay.

Therapist: When I can't program something . . .

Henry: When I can't program something I'm out of control. When I can't program something I'm not doing good for other people.

Therapist: When I gripe about my supervisor, I might mean . . .

Henry: When I gripe about my supervisor, I might mean I'm a lot like her. When I gripe about my supervisor, I might mean, "How dare you tell me what to do."

Therapist: Would you say that again.

Henry (obviously agitated at this point): How dare she tell me what to do.

Therapist: If I ever told my supervisor what I really felt . . .

Henry: If I ever told my supervisor how I really felt, I don't know what she'd do. If I ever told my supervisor what I really felt, she'd probably laugh. If I ever told my supervisor what I really felt, whatever she did she'd probably enjoy it.

Therapist: The uncertainty of my relationship with her . . .

Henry: The uncertainty of my relationship with her is that I haven't made it clear where I am at. The uncertainty of my relationship with her is that I've never laid it on the line.

Therapist: My supervisor's controlling me reminds me of . . .

Henry: My supervisor's controlling me reminds me of . . . (becoming more agitated) . . . my mother.

Therapist: Would you say that again?

Henry: My mother. My supervisor's controlling me reminds me of my mother.

Therapist: If I ever get it sorted out with mother . . .

56

Henry: If I ever get it sorted out with mother, I'd have to stand up to some things.

Therapist: My difficulties with my supervisor might be an avoidance of . . .

Henry: My difficulties with my supervisor might be an avoidance of, you know, my mother.

(At this point I wanted to shift Henry's focus to where his own words were leading him as I fed his thoughts back to him: an unresolved problem with his mother.)

Therapist: I can remember . . .

Henry: I can remember her hurting me. I can remember her seducing me. I can remember her (pause) giving me things to do that . . . (begins to cry) . . .

Therapist: One thing that's painful to remember is . . .

Henry: One thing that's painful to remember is how little I really know her.

Therapist: I'm becoming aware . . .

Henry: I'm becoming aware of how painful that is. I'm becoming aware of the fear.

Therapist: How do you feel right now?

Henry: I don't know. Kind of funny. A little dizzy.

Therapist: Do you want to go any further with this?

Henry: Yes, I do.

(I had been tempted to stop there because, although Henry had experienced a certain amount of emotion and come to some understanding, he still seemed rather distant from his own feelings, as if he were an observer rather than an emoting person. When he agreed to continue, I chose next to lead him into a fantasy where his feelings would be free to run their own course without his having to think them away. After several minutes spent trying to relax him in a comfortable position, I went on.)

Therapist: Imagine yourself riding along an expressway in a car. The steering goes out and the car crashes into an abutment, causing a terrible accident. You wake up in a hospital. You are very seriously injured, so seriously that you know you are going to die. You are beyond pain. You are going to die and you know it. You have only a few minutes to live. And just then your mother walks into the room. This is your very last chance to say whatever you haven't said. You have only a few minutes to talk to her, but whatever is unsaid will remain unsaid forever. *Be* in that hospital room. Stay in the fantasy. See your mother walk over to the bed. Speak to her.

Henry: Well, you know, mother, I just don't know what to say to you . . .

Therapist: Your very *last* chance, Henry.

Henry: I've really had it. (Sobbing) To you? I don't know what to say. There's nothing to say . . .

(Henry was obviously struggling against the feelings of pain and sadness that were beginning to well up in him. His body flinched slightly, nervously; his voice was almost a mumble. On the one hand, he was trying to let what he felt emerge; on the other, he was trying to shut it down. But he remained in the fantasy, continuing to talk to his image of his mother.)

Henry: It really sucks, this whole thing. You never read to me. You made me be too good. I don't know. (Loud sobbing and indistinct words) Shit! I wish to fuck you could just open up to me for a moment. (Crying louder) Why didn't you care? I reached out. Why didn't anything come back? (Pause. . . . trembling noticeably)

Therapist: Time is running out, Henry. Whatever you've left to say had better be said now.

Henry: You're a bitch. I want you to go. Why weren't you *there*? (ceases his loud crying and begins to whimper, like a child) Mommy . . . Mommy.

Therapist: Your very last moment. She's looking at you.

Henry: Why are you staring at me like that? (Pause) Mommy, I need you. Mommy, please . . .

(There was a long pause. Henry was beginning to relax, and appeared almost about to go to sleep. The emotions of pain, longing, sadness, and anger— evident to the group, though somewhat difficult to gather simply from his words—had peaked and subsided.)

Therapist: All right. Let the fantasy fade. Breathe slowly and deeply. That's it. Let your body relax and the fantasy dissolve. Relax a moment. Let yourself return, gradually, to this room, to this time, to this place. That's it. Breathe slowly and deeply. Very good. . . . How do you feel?

Henry: I feel *good*.

(Henry was smiling now, and much calmer. It was time to back away from his emotions and relate them to his judgments.)

Therapist: I have a sense here of what I call recapitulation. It seems to be a situation where you get yourself into a current bind because of unresolved past events. I'm talking about your relationship now with your supervisor. You seem to be using that to make your past come out all right. Particularly your relationship with your mother. You are upset because you cannot get it sorted out with your supervisor, but the real issue underneath is that you have not yet sorted it out with your mother. So your supervisor catches an awful lot more than she deserves. I had a sense when you were doing the role-playing that your supervisor wasn't such a bad lot at all, not nearly as bad as you had described her before. I had a sense that there was something else going on underneath that. There *had* to be *something*

59

else going on underneath that. There had to be something more. Then it became clear, from your own words, that it had something to do with your mother. And the tremendous anxiety and pain stirred up was all out of proportion to the way you were answering the sentence-completions before you got around to your mother.

Henry: Uh huh, uh huh. (In obvious agreement)

Therapist: I am pleased with how seriously you took everything. Not like you at all, is it? You'd prefer somebody else to do the work for you. But you got into it deeply, and all I had to do was follow. We're getting somewhere, I think, because you've finally decided to take the reins. (To Mike, who was role-playing with Henry earlier) Do you want to respond?

Mike: Well, I relate a lot to it, to this "recapitulation" as you called it. I know I do the same thing. I tried to be serious in the role-playing. I know I joke around a lot, but I did try to be serious this time, and it's a relief to find out it did some good.

Therapist: I suspect the reason you wanted to work with Henry is that the two of you are not so very different.

Mike: You can say that again.

Therapist: Anyone else like to respond?

(Several of the others made comments, but Henry was becoming restless. He wasn't paying much attention to what the others were saying and began more and more to interrupt them. Then he told us a dream.)

Henry: Not too long ago I had this dream about my supervisor. It was a funny dream and I'd like to talk about it. The first scene was like I was walking down a street and it was kind of dark around. There were a lot of buildings around, and I was talking with another person. We were rushing someplace. There was hardly any light, very dim, street-lights maybe, but that's all.

60

And the next scene is this gal (the supervisor), and she's sitting in kind of a gallery with people. And, you know, the background is kind of smoky and dark colored, and she takes off the top that she has on and exposes her breasts. She's sitting there, and well, it's more like her breasts are made-up, unreal. I mean she has a lot of cake makeup on them, red and pink, and her whole chest is inviting. And in real life, she's pretty tiny, you know, not very much filled out at all. But here her breasts are enormous.

Therapist: You said "inviting." Do you mean she's offering you her breasts?

Henry: Yeah, and she's got a big smile on her face.

Therapist: A big smile on her face with phony breasts?

Henry: Yeah.

Therapist: What does that remind you of?

Henry: (Deep sigh) Yeah.

Therapist: Didn't you say in the fantasy, "I have reached out to mother but nothing has come back?"

Henry: Yeah.

Therapist: Didn't you as a child feel you got a fake tit?

Henry: Yeah. (much more relaxed now)

Therapist: This seems a verification of what you just did. This is what you're hassling with this gal. You reach out, and nothing comes back.

Henry: Uh huh.

Therapist: And then you find the made-up breasts. She's inviting you to go to them, but they're unreal, fake, painted. Wasn't that your relationship to your mother? You said your mother "seduced" you. "Come close, come closer, but there's nothing here that is real. It's all made up." Which is a very, very painful thing for a child. For you.

Henry: She does it in such subtle little ways, you know.

Therapist: That's the dream. It's subtle. The breasts are

61

there, but they're painted, puffed up bigger than life. Did your mother ever perhaps offer you more than she produced?

Henry: Yeah, *yeah*. A helluva lot. She still does it all the time.

Therapist: I think if you can get in touch with that . . . I mean, "Don't keep trying to nurse a plastic breast." That's the message of the dream, or can you see something else in it?

Henry: No, that's pretty much how I felt.

Therapist: And I think the dream says essentially what you were saying in your fantasy and in your sentence-completions, and to some extent in your role-playing as well. It's a horrible thing for an infant to reach for a breast that offers less than is promised. But if you can face the fact that this woman, your boss, may be offering things more genuinely and straightforwardly than your mother did, I don't think you need to hassle with her for the wrong reasons.

Henry: Oh, uh huh, yes. I can see that sure enough.

Therapist: I'd like you to take this tape home and listen to it, listen to what you said and remember what you felt. Get the sense of it and bring back your response to it all. Are you willing to do that?

Henry: Yes, I'd like to. Very much.

Henry's session was just a beginning of course, but a positive one. As his relationship with his supervisor improved and his hostility towards his mother became clearer, he was able to look at the ways in which he was punishing himself by programming his own failures and laying the blame on others. But most important of all, he had learned how his own imagination can show him what he feels about his thoughts, and what he thinks about his feelings.

62

CHAPTER FIVE

FEAR

Of all the human feelings, fear is the one perhaps most often found to lie at the source of mental discomfort, hidden beneath layers of other feelings. Nonetheless, it has characteristics all its own which surface clearly from time to time and deserve attention.

The main ingredient of fear is expectation of some hurt or pain. Fear, more than any other emotion, is a kind of alarm system. It alerts us to an imminent danger, telling us that some harm is near. As such, there is nothing unhealthy about it. Indeed, if we had no way of assessing approaching danger, we would be at the mercy of any predator or danger. Fear is the danger signal that our security is being threatened. To the extent that we have learned to be afraid of situations, persons, and events that are in fact dangerous, fear provokes appropriate protective responses. To the extent that we have learned to be afraid of nondangerous situations, persons, and events, our fear will provoke overprotective measures which can only be self-defeating in the long run. None of us, of course, is without such irrational fears. But neither need we be unwilling to face their unreasonableness and question it. In practice, most of us prefer to keep looking for ways to reduce fear, rather than to investigate it and find healthy and reasonable ways of coping with it.

FEAR OF THE FORGOTTEN
One of the most common and most neglected forms of

irrational, counterproductive fear is that rooted in "forgotten memories." The following excerpt from a group therapy session illustrates the process dramatically. Debbie was a seventeen-year-old girl who held a part-time job at a supermarket where she ran a cash register at the check-out counter. She complained of becoming excessively frightened when her boss would come by periodically to see how she was doing. She felt that his surveillance was fair and reasonable, but still found herself getting upset at his approach and making an unusual number of mistakes. After she had discussed the problem for a while, I made the following suggestion:

Therapist: Is there someone willing to play the role of Debbie?

Peter: I will.

Therapist: Fine. Don't be too critical, Debbie, of how Peter role-plays you. But you play the boss. I want to get some sense of how he handled the situation. Just accept Peter's version of you for the time being and be more concerned with your accuracy in portraying the boss. Okay?

Debbie: Okay.

(I was using the role-playing device both to gather further information and to try to determine what emotions were interfering with Debbie's performance at work.)

Therapist: Now give me the scene, Debbie.

Debbie: Okay, Peter, you stand here behind the check-out counter. And I'll be the boss buying stuff from you.

Therapist: Right, and he gets upset and gives you a dollar extra change. Have I got it right? Okay, you two take it from here.

Peter: Well, here's your change, sir. 10, 20, 30, 40, and

one dollar. And how much did you give me? Oh yeah, 10, okay. There we are.

Debbie: Now you've just got to watch these mistakes, young lady. This is why I'm always coming out short at the end of the day.

Peter: I'm sorry, sir. I thought you gave me a 10, that's why I gave you the extra dollar. I'm sorry. I'm learning. It's just a little tricky. Do you have everything you wanted to buy?

Therapist: All right, let's stop there for now. Is that pretty much the scene?

Debbie: Yeah, that's it. Exactly. (Smiling)

Therapist: Peter, do you think you have a sense of how the boss handled that? Do you think you could play the boss? Okay, now just change places with Debbie. That's it. And this time, Debbie, you're going to play yourself and Peter will be your boss. Okay?

Debbie: Okay. Hi, George.

Peter: Hi, Debbie.

Debbie: Okay, $5.70. That's $6.70, $8.00, $9.00, $10.00, and thank you.

Peter: Thank *you*.

Debbie: Oops. Did I give you a dollar extra? I'm sorry.

Peter: You shouldn't be making that mistake any more—but you just did. That's our money, you know. You shouldn't be giving it away like that. 'Cause a lot of people, they'll just take it. But at least you caught it in time. Most people would've just walked out. Just watch it, you know.

Debbie: I understand.

(It is obvious at this point that Debbie is getting emotional. I interrupt.)

Therapist: What's going on with you, Debbie, right now?

Debbie: I feel sort of funny. I don't feel good. I feel stupid. (Starting to cry)

Therapist: Okay. I have something else in mind. I want you to become aware of how you feel. You feel stupid. Anything else?

Debbie: (Pause) I feel stupid . . . I feel dumb . . . I feel sad.

Therapist: Okay. What I want you to do is close your eyes and think back into your childhood to a time when you felt the way you feel now. I want you to think back to a particular instant in your childhood, a particular event when the feelings were the same as those you are now experiencing: feeling stupid, kind of embarassed, I suspect, feeling sad, incompetent. Okay, now would you just look at Peter and describe that?

(The role-playing has ended.)

Debbie: It's summer and I'm standing outside. (Pause)

Therapist: I want you to *be* there. Actually the way you're doing it is fine. Be there. You are standing outside. Go ahead.

Debbie: I'm doing work . . . in dirt. My family is outside. My dad's right there. And all of a sudden I look down and there's a green spider crawling on my arm and I start screaming loud. (Agitated and crying) I'm scared because I'm scared of spiders and I go to dad and say, "Dad, please get this spider off," and he goes, "No, you can get it off yourself." And I go, "No." (Screaming and obviously frightened) "It's going to hurt me. Get it off me!" He goes, "No, you can get it off yourself. Just go run upstairs and hit it off." And I run upstairs, and I'm just screaming because I'm so afraid- . . . so afraid I can't get it off.

Therapist: Let me talk to this little girl . . . How old are you, little girl?

Debbie: I'm about eight.

Therapist: About eight. Let me talk to you, little girl. (Pause) You seem frightened, little girl.

Debbie: Yeah.

Therapist: Tell me about it.

Debbie: I'm scared of spiders. A spider got on me.

Therapist: Why didn't you go talk to your father? He was right there.

Debbie: I asked him to get it off, but he said I could do it myself, but I couldn't.

Therapist: What happened?

Debbie: I was scared, crying. (Very low voice) Please, please, daddy.

Therapist: And he wouldn't help you?

Debbie: No, he told me to go do it by myself.

Therapist: And you couldn't?

Debbie: No . . . He told me to go by myself, he told me there was nothing to be afraid of, he told me I was stupid to be afraid.

Therapist: But you *were* scared. Spiders scared you an awful lot, and he told you not to be scared?

Debbie: Yeah.

Therapist: What does that do to you when he tells you you shouldn't be scared and you are?

Debbie: It makes me feel stupid. I feel like a baby.

Therapist: Like a baby, like you can't do it, like you're going to make mistakes. It seems to me, little girl—look at me—it seems to me that unless you figure this out it might cause you problems later on.

Debbie: Yeah.

Therapist: I wonder how, when you get older, you'll feel when you make mistakes. How do you think you'll feel.

Debbie: Afraid . . . and stupid.

Therapist: Afraid and stupid. (Pause) Breathe slowly now. Relax and let the fantasy fade away.

(Debbie had faced the feelings she had as a child. Further insight into her current behavior and her childhood memory could now take place. I opted at this point to make use of the Sentence-Completion Technique, using Peter, who was sitting opposite her, as her partner.)

Therapist: All right now, Debbie. Just look at Peter and complete each sentence I give you. Okay? "When I make a mistake at work . . ."

Debbie: When I make mistakes at work I'm afraid I'll get fired. When I make mistakes at work I feel silly. When I make mistakes at work I wish I could go hide.

Therapist: The way I learned to feel that way was . . .

Debbie: The way I learned to feel that way was when dad told me I was stupid for making mistakes. (Slight crying. . . . Pause.)

Therapist: I'm becoming aware . . .

Debbie: I'm becoming aware that my father doesn't like it when I make mistakes.

Therapist: Could you say that again?

Debbie: In order to make father correct I make myself feel stupid when I make mistakes.

Therapist: A better way might be . . .

Debbie: A better way might be to accept the mistakes and try to do better the next time.

Therapist: Would you say that again?

Debbie: A better way to do it might be to accept it and try harder the next time.

(At this point, hoping to secure Debbie's gains from the session with some practical activity, I make a suggestion.)

Therapist: One thing I can do this week to work on this problem might be . . .

Debbie: One thing I can do this week to work on this problem might be when George comes to my cash register again, just act natural like I would with any other customer.

Therapist: Just relax. Breathe slowly and relax. (Pause) How do you feel now?

Debbie: I feel a little nervous but I don't feel stupid any more. I feel like I understand better, and like I won't feel so dumb when I make another mistake.

Therapist: Good. I'd feel nervous too if I had to change the way you ought to change. I like what you did. I like it a lot and I have a real sense of your understanding it now. I think it's a very high price to pay to attempt to continue to please daddy by clobbering yourself that way. I think you're capable of leading your own life a little better. What do you think?

Debbie: I think so, too.

Therapist: Would you let me know what happens with your boss this coming week? I'd be very interested in finding out. How do you feel now?

Debbie: I don't feel sad any more.

(At this point I asked the group for their reactions.)

Therapist: Would you like to respond, Peter?

Peter: Yeah. I feel like I'm still in your boat, Debbie. I had a job where I gave a guy too much change and I was afraid of getting fired. And I still get nervous when I have to give change. But it seems so unnecessary to get scared. You're a lot smarter, you know, when you're not scared.

Therapist: That's a good way of putting it. You are a lot smarter, and you do deserve more than getting stuck in childhood fear. Does anyone else want to respond to Debbie?

Josh: Yeah. I felt really mad at her father. I can understand he was sort of, you know, trying to teach Debbie that it won't hurt you, but it seemed a helluva way to do it.

Therapist: It *is* a hell of a way to do it, isn't it. I mean, here's a little girl, very frightened, and her father says, "You're not *supposed* to be scared." But in fact she was terrified. Not only that, she was made to feel dumb about being terrified, and I find that cruel on the part of her father—unintentional, but cruel nonetheless. I think he was right, objectively, about the spider. But he certainly wasn't in tune with your panicky fear.

(Several more of the group responded with comments and questions and reflections from their own experience. When it was clear that the process had come to term, I turned one last time to Debbie.)

Therapist: Would you like to take the tape we made of this session and play it for your father, Debbie?

Debbie: Yeah, I would like that.

Therapist: Does anyone object if Debbie plays this tape for her father? . . . All right. I don't think it's necessary, Debbie, but you may if you want to. How do you feel now?

Debbie: Much better. I'm scared about playing it, but I think it's good.

Debbie returned a week later. She had played the tape for her parents and her father told her that he understood how his own feelings had unwittingly gotten in the way of his relationship to her. Debbie also reported, with obvious pleasure, that her boss had commended her on her improvement and on seeming less nervous at the cash register.

DISPLACING FEAR

Not every instance of misplaced fear is as clear and as easy to correct as Debbie's was. But her problem is typical, and illustrates how neglecting to investigate the source of fear limits the possibility of doing much about it. For fear survives its repression and can take the form of irrational and often counterproductive behavior, like misguided anger, psychosomatic illness, social mischief, sexual malfunction, etc. Since these things are generally easier to detect and deal with than underlying fears, one tends to overlook that they are symptoms rather than causes, and that the deeper fears will continue to produce new symptoms as fast as the old ones can be cured.

Frightened people often behave as if they were very angry: fearing helplessness, they make efforts to deny their vulnerability. The bully is a good example. For fear of being hurt, he will continually provoke fights with those weaker than himself in a futile attempt to prove to himself that he is not going to get hurt. Similarly, the violence of the nonstop talker, whose torrent of words drowns out everyone within range, may stem from a simple fear of not being noticed or not being listened to.

Alternatively, we may get angry at people we meet who appear to be frightened, often because they stir up memories of fears in ourselves that we have not adequately understood. The parent who ridicules a child for being a "scaredy-cat" is not only denying his own fear but is teaching the child to do the same. For it is altogether reasonable to be frightened if someone threatens us or forces us into unwilling submission. But if the fear itself is overpowered and denied expression, it tends to get displaced from its real object and to take on a life all its own, provoking symptoms far removed from its origins. In this way, for example, even the positive, affectionate response of another person who is reaching out to us and wants to get close can be terrifying in the extreme if we have been subjected to ridicule for our fear of taking risks. The fear of rejection can close us off from the warmest and most inviting affections of those about us, causing us to boil with anger or slink off in shyness, and so create the very rejection we most feared.

Fear, anger, and affection, then, are seldom what they seem, and their relationships to one another can get exceedingly complex. This is so because fear, anger, and affection are similar in that they can all have immediate objects of their own and can all be displaced onto secondary objects. What is more, they can all replace one another as symptoms in conditions where the appropriate emotional response has been blocked. Of the three, however, fear is usually the most disguised and detoured because it is by nature introverted and private. By contrast, anger and affection tend to be extroverted.

Think of yourself for a moment expressing anger. Picture yourself all physically charged up and tensed for action. Imagine what your breathing would be like, your stance, your movements, as you suddenly explode in frenzied, ferocious violence, striking out at the person or object that has provoked you. If you imagine in a similar fantasy the conditions constellated when you express affection, you note a change in the physical reactions and in your state of mind. But you also observe that the emotion only comes to term when you have reached the object of your feelings.

But now imagine yourself very frightened, horrified. Conjure up some image of a terrifying situation and observe what happens to your body in the fantasy. Your breathing becomes shallow and confined mostly to the upper chest. You draw back and want to curl up inside of yourself to hide. (The more vivid your imagination, the more these very conditions can be created by the fantasy itself.) Now imagine the frightening person or object passing you by without noticing you. Your body loosens, your breathing becomes more regular and full. You get a grip on yourself and can carry on as before.

Because fear is an *implosive* (bursting inward) emotion—unlike anger and affection, which are *explosive* (bursting outward)—it causes us to shrink within ourselves. It is the most troublesome of the basic emotions. Lacking the expressive safety valves of anger and affection, it gets trapped within us. Fear is also the most difficult emotion to deal with in a therapeutic situation since it is the one the individual is most generally unwilling to face. Feelings of fear are those we are most apt to deny, and, failing that, to make excuses for. We will do almost anything, it seems, to protect ourselves from taking responsibility for our fear, which makes symptomatic displacement inevitable and often dangerously uncontrollable.

DEALING WITH FEAR

Several years ago, while working in a mental hospital, I witnessed a powerful example of the force of pent-up fear. A woman patient, who was being assisted back to her room by one of the aides, suddenly got the idea that he was arresting her against her will. She struck out at him, and three more aides rushed to the rescue (her outbreaks of aggression were notorious in the ward). The woman only grew more violent and finally another two aides were called for. It required six grown, rather husky men to subdue this one woman, who weighed no more than 130 pounds. During the struggle she literally picked up an aide with one hand and threw him to the floor so violently that several of the bones in one arm were shattered—and that while all six of them were trying to contain her. Such unusual strength is made possible by a rapid redistribution of body hormones; but it must also be seen as the force of internalized terror abruptly exploding into panic. It is the strength of the small animal protecting its young from a predator. It is the strength of a man lifting up a car to free his trapped child. It is the strength of a personality instinctively frightened of losing itself in institutionalized therapy lashing out blindly in every direction.

Panic is not as a rule a very efficient way of dealing with fear or its objects. Where self-protective violence seems required to ward off oppression, calculated rage is a better weapon. Recently, in Chicago, a woman was approached by a would-be rapist. She did not panic, but calmly and apparently willingly yielded to his advances. "You don't have to force me like this," she informed her assailant, "I like it." Her words threw the man off guard enough for the woman to reach unseen into her handbag for a razor. He didn't notice until his penis was cut off. He bled to death in a hospital emergency room. There is no reason to doubt the woman's fear simply because she was able to convert it into a calculated attack. Rather—rightly or wrongly—her fear was effective in warding off danger precisely because it did not become displaced in panic.

Both cases are extreme ways of dealing with fear, but carry an important message. Most of us, it is true, do not get panic-striken or enraged when faced with frightening situations. We are more apt to be like Debbie and bury fears beneath less violent symptoms. Indeed, we may even deny the possibility of ever giving way to such panic or rage. Dealing with fear maturely, however, begins with recognizing both its *existence* and its *force*.

ESCAPING FROM FEAR

Of the myriad possibilities for escaping from the existence and force of fear rather than dealing with them maturely, three can be singled out as illustrative examples: submissiveness, sensuality, and seduction. In each of them we can see the same dangerous process at work: exchanging the difficult responsibility of fear for more manageable responsibilities.

Submissiveness enables us to deny our fears and to protect ourselves against them by playing into what others want of us. The "good" child, the "good" wife, and the "good" employee, who identify being good with adjusting to the expectations of their superiors, are all examples of people attempting to protect themselves against fear of rejection. By always doing "the proper thing," an individual assures himself of a minimal, though ultimately unsatisfying, acceptance by others. I remember one man I saw in therapy whose fear of being rejected by his mother kept him tied to her and seemed to inhibit any depth of relationship with his peers. His explanation was curious: "If I ever told my mother of all the things I've done in my life, it would kill her. She'd die if she knew how I was behaving. I don't want to hurt her, so I won't tell her." By locating the problem mistakenly in secret disobediences, he exchanged the fear of rejection for the easier fear of being found out. When he decided at last to confess his failure to her, his mother's response was less one of shock than of relief that her submissive son had finally made some effort to stand on his own. In removing the protection, he was able to face his in fact unreasonable fears of rejection lying behind it.

Sensuality is another frequent device for escaping fear, and this it does by restricting the individual's attention to the task of satisfying selected physical needs. The Don Juans who maintain a series of simultaneous sexual adventures in order to avoid their fears of intimacy, and the suburban hypochondriacs who organize their day around trips to the medicine cabinet in order to screen fears of deeper psychological maladjustment, are both instances of this mechanism at work.

75

But perhaps the most insidious and yet most common form of denying fear is *seduction*. Seduction exchanges the fear of failure for the fear of getting caught at mistakes. The seductive individual never discovers his resources and talents because he refuses to accept the final responsibility for any context in which they could be tested. He does whatever possible to con the graces and ability of others and to maneuver their successes and failure to his own advantage. The seducer is one of the most difficult patients to treat in therapy because his unusually low level of self-reliance makes him particularly resistant to change.

Escaping fear in any fashion does not eliminate it any more than closing one's eyes makes one invisible. In fact, the more we deny our feelings, the more control we relinquish to them. The fear whose original object is forgotten is set at liberty to distract other feelings from their proper objects and to confuse our efforts at self-determination. No life worth living can afford to deny the fear which no life is without.

CHAPTER SIX

ANGER

Anger, like fear, is an emotion. So obvious a fact would hardly seem worth mentioning, were it not so often missing from the ideas people carry around with them about anger. An emotion is a felt impulse to act in a certain way, based on a judgment about something perceived. Whereas with fear we feel like escaping from something we judge to be dangerous, with anger we feel like attacking and destroying it. The first thing to notice about being angry, then, is that we *feel like* doing something.

Now the feeling is distinct from what we actually do about it. Between the impulse and the act stands a choice. This point is important, because we grow accustomed to the leap from feeling like doing something out of anger to thinking that actually doing it is inevitable as long as the feeling persists. But emotions are not choices and do not deserve to be treated as such. Stifling an emotional impulse to action is not a choice against the action but against the impulse. We choose *not* to choose by removing the feeling which puts us in a position of forced option. Because of unfortunate learning experiences, we may not realize that the range of possible behaviorial expressions of anger is as broad as for any other emotion. And so it is that we too often prefer to avoid the very feeling of doing something we judge immoral or inappropriate, rather than to respect the feeling and its underlying perceptual judgment by seeking alternate forms of expression for it.

THE NATURAL ORIGINS OF ANGER

In order further to clarify the nature of anger and to isolate its particular functions, we may begin by looking at its origins.

Anger is a natural and spontaneous feeling-response to an obstacle perceived as threatening to an individual's line of action. If something is in my way and I wish it were not, I feel angry. I can no more *decide* to feel angry than I can decide to feel hungry. In the same way that I can decide when to eat and when not to eat if I get hungry, so too I can decide what to do or what not to do if I get angry. But I cannot in truth say, "I will not feel angry," any more than I can say, "I will not feel hungry." Once the natural conditions for a feeling have been constellated, there is no refusing its appearance. It is automatic.

On the other hand, it *is* true that as I learn to deal effectively with my anger and to understand its natural origins, situations that may once have provoked strong anger can come to excite me less, or perhaps not at all. But this is because I have learned to modify my judgments. For example, I used to get furious when another motorist would cut me off at an intersection. Then I recognized that my disproportionate anger was prompted more by my competitiveness and lack of concern for others than by an appreciation of the objective danger of the situation. As a result, I have since become more willing to yield the right-of-way to the other driver, even though he may not legally own it. His cutting me off need no longer be construed as a personal failure on my part, though this does not preclude my getting angry at careless drivers who threaten the safety of others. In both cases, my feelings reflected the state of my judgments. In reassessing them and reinterpreting the situation, my feelings changed accordingly.

Take another example. You are on a crowded bus and someone steps on your foot. You feel immediate but minimal anger and turn to ask the offender kindly to watch his step. But when you turn, you notice that he is wearing dark glasses and carrying a white cane. Your feelings change at once. You no longer feel angry, because you no longer feel you have been carelessly tramped on. Conversely, if you turn to discover that someone intentionally, rather than accidentally, stepped on your foot, you will become even more angry, because you would judge the situation more severely than at first.

Once we recognize that the natural origins of feeling angry lie in our interpretations of situations, we can better appreciate that anger cannot be controlled *directly*. Repeating over and over again, "I am not angry, I am not angry" will not make the feeling go away. If anything, one will grow more angry, since the very refusal itself only reinforces the perceptions which excited the anger. Anger can only be controlled *indirectly*, by altering judgment.

THE ETHICAL NEUTRALITY OF ANGER

Like the other emotions, anger is ethically neutral. Many of us grew up under the mistaken conviction that certain feelings are somehow immoral. But feeling afraid or sexually aroused is no more morally "bad" than feeling happy and content is morally "good." Morality is determined by what we *do*, not by how we *feel*. It is how we express our anger that may be judged morally right or wrong. It may be considered morally wrong to kill someone who angers me; but it cannot be morally wrong to feel angry enough at him to want to do so. It is only a short step from judging that anger is immoral to judging ourselves to be evil because we feel angry. The mother who is frequently angry with her child may begin to judge herself to be a bad mother because she cannot control the anger she feels towards the child. All the more readily may she judge herself to be an evil person because of the fantasies that occur to her of wishing the child might die in his sleep to bring her some peace of mind. Once ethical sanctions have been placed on feelings, it is little wonder that we make an effort to deny or restrain them. For instance, a child may become so angry at his father that he would like to shoot him, and even begin imagining how he might do it. But if he has been taught that he is not *supposed* to feel that way towards his father, or that it is *bad* to feel angry, he will learn to repress the feelings, and in so doing likely only complicate matters by harboring feelings of guilt besides. A child is as entitled to his anger as he is to his feelings of fear, sadness, disappointment, and joy. He must be taught to distinguish what he feels from what he does about it; but if he is taught that certain feelings are taboo, he must perforce devise ways of denying them or live with a distorted image of himself as immoral for having feelings he "ought not" be having.

Just as anger is not morally evil, neither can it be inappropriate. No activity or individual or situation enjoys the right of being an improper object of anger. Fathers and mothers sometimes try to assume such a privileged position in their children's eyes. Where this is the case, a parent will refuse to attend to the feeling behind an angry statement, insisting rather on its impropriety: "Don't talk to us like that. We're your parents." It may well be that the child's choice of words is offensive, but if the parent does not at least recognize the anger that prompted the statement, he will be teaching the child to distrust communicating what he feels. Conversely, parents often become worried when they feel angry at their children, falsely assuming that parents should "love" their children without ever getting angry, because they have accepted a romanticized picture of family life that makes angry feelings inappropriate. When a small child has a new baby brother, he feels understandably upset and gets angry. Mother tells him, "You shouldn't feel that way. He's your new baby brother." If the child could sort out his perceptual judgments, he might reply: "Yes, I know. That's why I'm angry. I didn't ask for him and I don't want him. I had things going pretty well for me until he came along." And the mistake is spread around to other family relations. Grandmother comes over and wants a big hug and kiss from five-year-old Suzie. Suzie does not particularly like Grandmother and would rather be outside with her friends anyway. She feels like kicking Grandmother in the shins, but just stomps her feet on the floor instead. Mother says, "Now, Suzie, you shouldn't feel that way. Go on and give Grandmother a big kiss. Remember the doll she brought you on your birthday. She *is* your grandmother, you know." And so Suzie goes through the ritual, learning in its course the art of hiding how she feels.

Anger is not immature. Becoming an adult has nothing at all to do with feeling or not feeling angry. What we are angry about and how we deal with our anger does change as we mature, but the capacity for feeling anger is never lost. There are certain expressions of anger that are immature, to be sure. Throwing a temper tantrum—that is, using a dramatic expression of anger to force others against their will to conform to what we want—is childish. On the other hand, being able to control expressions of anger under certain circumstances is requisite to adult behavior. For instance, I am at a meeting where it is important to complete certain business transactions. I become angry at the way a particular individual is disrupting things by trying to interject humorous comments at every juncture. I know at whom I am angry and why, but decide that for the sake of preventing any further delay I will keep the expression of my feelings to myself. This is not denying them and so does not inhibit me, should matters get too far out of hand, from expressing them openly.

Finally, anger is not undignified or beastly. Part of the mystique of mass media "idols" is the association set up between their ability to remain calm in all situations and so to triumph over the emotional rabble. The dignified restraint of anger is, in this way, projected as a tool for control and power over others, while "losing control of oneself" is construed as "acting like an animal." But acting humanly is surely defined more by how we treat ourselves and others than by the selection of which feelings to express. Learning to trust *all* our feelings and to integrate them into the meaning we give the things of our life is essential to the fullness of humanity, and better enables us to choose to care for one another and ourselves with the esteem we deserve. Anger is no exception to this rule.

FEAR OF ANGER

There are certain fears about expressing anger that lead us to shun feeling it. Two of them can be singled out as fundamental.

The first we have already mentioned in passing: the fear that emotions of anger signal evil traits of character. The underlying assumption is that good people simply do not feel angry. But good people—the very best—obviously do. Many of our most esteemed cultural and spiritual giants were persons of tremendous creative wrath. Even our traditional heroes of nonviolence—like Jesus, Gandhi, and Martin Luther King—are people whose very nobility was revealed in their unrelenting fury against injustice and oppression. Consider the rage of Jesus: "Just before the Jewish Passover, Jesus went up to Jerusalem, and in the temple he found the people selling cattle and sheep and pigeons, and the money-changers sitting at the counter there. Making a whip out of some cord, he drove them all out of the temple, cattle and sheep as well, scattered the money-changers' coins, knocked the tables over, and said to the pigeon-sellers, 'Take all this out of here and stop turning my father's house into a market' " (John 2, 14-6). Like the protests of Gandhi and the demonstrations of Dr. King, Jesus's dramatic action was aimed not so much at the individuals who were carrying on customs they had inherited from the ancestors, but at the institutions which had taken away responsibilities that belonged to them, and which had distorted their actions into a betrayal of the ideals they professed. And all of them were angry, very angry, men.

A second fear, no less unreasonable than the first, is that anger always means rejection. Not everyone who gets angry at me necessarily intends to reject me; nor do I always have to reject a person with whom I am angry. It is entirely possible—and usually more mature as well—to restrict anger to some aspect of an individual's behavior without generalizing it to a judgment about the individual himself. What tends to make the distinction difficult for many people is that anger has in fact meant rejection, often deep and abiding rejection, by those on whose love they had come to depend. Young children are particularly vulnerable here because of the difficulty they have in distinguishing what they are from what they do. Thus when a parent directs anger at something the child does, the child may perceive this as a total rejection. And the way the parent expresses the anger may confirm the message. "Get out of this house with those muddy shoes. And don't you come back," shouts the mother to her little son who had just tracked mud across the shag rug. What she *wanted* to communicate was her anger with the child for walking into the living room without changing his shoes. What she may *in fact* have communicated was that he did not deserve to live in the same home with her any longer. There are also cases of genuine, intentional rejection out of anger—as for example that of the tribal chief's son, described earlier—and their impressions can be traumatic, if not nearly incorrigible, in later life.

What is important to remember in all of this, however, is that fear of anger is always a dangerous and ultimately self-defeating posture. Indeed, deprived of anger, a person is deprived of one of the greatest gifts his nature has provided him to discern a lack of care and be moved to correct it.

MISCONSTRUING ANGER

Since the judgments that ground feelings are usually quite complex tangles of perceptions and interpretations, it is easy to understand why almost every feeling-state is a compound of various emotions difficult to sort out from one another. This not only means that how we deal with any particular emotional impulse tends to affect other companion impulses, but also that we may confuse the expression of one feeling with the expression of another. Much of our fear about feeling angry can be traced back to misconstruing anger and its expressions.

Being angry is not the same thing as being sad. The affliction or regret over loss which we sense in sadness *may* be felt along with anger in a given situation, but need not necessarily be present. Hence the common attempt to avoid anger in order to "feel happy" is an abuse of feeling based on the misunderstanding that anger entails sadness.

Nor is being angry the same as being depressed. Depression does always involve anger—indeed, deep, penetrating anger—but anger does not always involve depression. Anger can lead to an expression of hope just as easily as to the submissive resignation of the choice to be depressed.

To be angry does not mean to hate. Hatred is an impulse informing a chosen moral judgment about someone or something; anger is based on a spontaneous perceptual judgment. Anger can express itself in hatred. But it can also be expressed in benevolent and affectionate ways alien to hatred. Hate is the very antithesis of the choice to care, since it has already decided on the worthlessness of its object. It is particularly important for children to be taught the difference between the two. Yet too often parents presume that the child already knows it, and so end up moralizing about his anger instead of about his hatred. "I hate you" is often simply a child's confused way of saying, "I am angry with you." Left too long unchallenged, the association of anger with hatred can be a difficult pattern to break in later life.

Anger is not rage—be it blind or calculated—though it is an essential element to all rage. One can react to anger by allowing the emotional impulses absolute control in immediate, irrational rage or panic. One can just as easily choose to direct one's anger in reasoned, perhaps even violent, rage against its object. In either case, feeling angry does not demand becoming enraged.

Finally, anger is closely related to, and often confused with, fear. Anger accompanies or even displaces fear when escape from the object perceived as dangerous has been cut off. A frightened animal that has been cornered is a good example of this process. Unable to hide and unwilling to submit, it will become vicious and attack, even though its aggressor be many times more powerful. Its fear of being hurt is turned into self-defense by the addition of anger.

Humans respond in a similar fashion. A frightened person who feels trapped is likely to become angry and defensive. It may not always be easy to determine *why* a person feels hemmed in, but his self-defensive anger assures us that somehow he *does*. Like the animal, he is protecting himself from being hurt. By understanding the relationships between fear, anger, and hurt, we can avoid being drawn into unnecessary battles or provoking them ourselves. On the other hand, if we have learned that showing fear is always cowardly and ridiculous, we are more likely to ward off fear by expressing anger. And if others respond to this confusion of emotions, they confirm the misinterpretation that lies behind it. Only when a person discovers that he can express his fear before another without being taken advantage of will he be able to uncover the hurt that first generated his feeling.

DISPLACING ANGER

The force of an emotional impulse of anger, if denied, is turned against the feeling subject in a self-destructive fashion. Neglected anger builds up and remains hidden only so long as the mechanisms of denial can withstand it. When the pressure becomes too great, it breaks out in displacement on secondary objects.

First of all, the body may become the object of one's aggressions. Psychosomatic illness, as we noted in an earlier chapter, is a particularly dangerous form of displacement because it has the appearance of a purely physiological disorder and does not immediately inform the individual of a breakdown in his defenses.

A second form of escaping anger and then falling prey to it ourselves is seen in so-called passive-aggressive activity. As the name suggests, aggression is released under the guise of passivity. The same effect is secured as if one had expressed the anger openly, it seems. But in fact, by erecting a facade of innocence to avoid the stigma of displaying anger, the person only further denies responsibility for his feelings and alienates himself from those who become the object of his passive aggressions. Instead of telling someone

I am angry about having to take him to the store, I arrive late to pick him up. Instead of telling the principal I am angry at being assigned an extra class, I do a poor job of teaching it. Instead of telling my father I am angry at his putting me through college, I flunk out in the first year. The possibilities of passive-aggressive response are endless. And with each new displacement of anger, the pattern etches deeper and deeper into character.

Finally, anger may be displayed indirectly in the apparently forthright expression of other feelings. Sexual relationships are the frequent scenes of such displacement. A woman may sexually seduce a man—or vice versa—out of anger, exposing him to ridicule or contempt, at least in her own eyes. Alternatively, she may become frigid with a man to avenge herself of the times that he, or other men, have treated her badly. Chronic complaining and irritability is another such ruse: the totally indiscrimate search for imperfections, great or small, in everyone and everything. These judgments soon fall into distortions of the facts, since they are not concerned with correcting what is wrong, but only with venting anger once-removed from its original perceptual judgments. A cartoon I once saw pictured it perfectly. A disgruntled man sat crouched deep in a chair with a dark, stormy cloud hanging over his head. His wife, standing off to one side, was remarking to a friend: "Whatever it is, George is against it. It keeps him going."

Because anger *can* be misunderstood, pent up, and displaced, and so often *is*, does not mean it *must be*. Anger can just as easily be expressed constructively and lead to an increase of insight and love, of communication and creative conflict. Like the marvelous lance of Achilles which could at once mortally wound a foe and heal a wounded friend, anger can be used to whatever purpose we direct it. It needs to be respected, not hidden away. It needs care, which alone can transform anger and drive out fear.

CHAPTER SEVEN

PAIN

The first thing to understand about pain is that it *is painful*. No one really enjoys it. No matter what explanation we find for our pain, no matter what other pleasures it heightens, no matter what greater good we suppose it to serve, it is still pain. Worse still, nothing seems to bring more pain than trying to avoid it altogether.

Biologically viewed, pain is a signal that something is wrong, that some maladjustment of our physical apparatus to its environment has occurred which needs correction. The same thing is true of emotional or psychological pain, which can complicate physical pain with those afflictions of spirit that signal the maladjustment of some aspect of our behavior to the things we value.

Unfortunately, in both cases we too often become preoccupied with dismissing the painful feeling and forget about what it is supposed to alert us to. The worst thing that can happen, therefore, is that these superficial devices for alleviating pain actually take effect. The maladjustment is then forced to seek other secondary, and more painful, signals which are less likely to be heeded than the original pain, and so to preoccupy us only further with adjusting how we feel rather than determining what is wrong with us.

PHYSICAL PAIN

All of us know only too well the experience of physical pain: the knee we skinned at hopscotch, the bone we broke in high school gym class, the appendix that ruptured on a transatlantic flight. When we are in deep physical pain, we spontaneously reach for the quickest available relief. But sometimes we are forced to entrust ourselves to the care of someone else who, in order to get to the cause of the discomfort, has to cause us still greater pain: the draining and drilling of an abscessed tooth, the setting of a dislocated shoulder, and even the removal of a splinter are all examples of this. That men struggle to find ways to correct the causes of pain painlessly is hardly to be wondered at. Like the old alchemists in the quest for the elixir of life, medical science—as often distinct from the medical industries—has as its ideal *the relief of all pain and its causes.*

But imagine, for a moment, that whenever we were in pain we could somehow magically *wish* it away, without having to do anything further about it. Think of what would happen. Most of us would take advantage of such a power so often that we would soon do ourselves serious organic damage. The tooth would never be filled, the shoulder would remain permanently dislocated, the infection would never heal. We would have no defense at all against disease, paralysis, and death. Imagine further a man who could wish that magical wish once and for all, and never have to feel pain again. He would not even know when he was hurt. Scalding water and broken glass would be no threat to him. But he would need a twenty-four-hour guardian to make sure he did not injure or kill himself, since he would have no means himself of determining that his body needed attention. The painless state of that man would be worse than the painful one.

When a dentist tells a child about to have a cavity drilled, "This won't hurt," he sets up a reflex reaction which only makes the child feel the pain more intensely. The fact is, it *will* hurt. And the lie—far from achieving the dentist's goal of communicating his good intentions and relaxing the child—confirms in the child a distrust of authority and of his own capacity to withstand pain. It is, after all, possible to care for people in pain without denying the pain or placing the blame on them for what they feel.

Several years ago, on a Sunday afternoon, I was hiking with my wife and two children in the country. My son, then six-years-old, slipped and cut the back of his head rather badly. He was bleeding profusely and it looked like he had broken a large blood vessel. We drove to the nearest town, some fifteen miles away, and found a doctor. After washing the wound and assessing the damage, the doctor prepared a needle and sutures. My son, already in pain and frightened by the gushing blood, asked me if it would hurt. I told him that it would hurt, very much; that it was all right for him to cry; but that it would help if he could try to keep his head still. I also told him that I was going to help the doctor by holding his head; that the whole thing would take about five or ten minutes; and that it was important, even though I did not like it anymore than he. A few minutes later, I told my son it was all over and that the pain would lessen over the next hour or so. His response was: "Can we finish our hike now? It still hurts a little, but not that much." Later that evening we talked about the discomfort, and the value of pain in helping us know what to do.

EMOTIONAL PAIN

Physical pain is, in great part, unavoidable. It does not need any welcome to find its way to us, but it can be appropriated into the meaning we give our lives. This is no less true for emotional pain. Sadness, grief, longing, loneliness, and remorse are part of our very humanity, and should be allowed to alert us that something needs changing or that something which cannot be changed needs accepting.

It is more difficult to deal directly with emotional pain

90

and its causes than with physical pain. But it is also more dangerous not to. Neglecting to take responsibility for our emotional pain is to surrender our capacity for self-determination to symptoms and syndromes which may easily develop into complete depression. Of this we shall have more to say in the next chapter. For the moment, we need only note that emotional pain itself is not nearly as harmful as the denial of it. However disguised the blessings of such pain, they are not to be overlooked. In the last analysis, emotional pain is the psyche's attempt to heal itself, and we can choose either to contribute to that process or to impede it.

Far sadder than seeing people adrift in a sea of painful emotions is watching them cling desperately to every passing twig and branch while they await rescue—when most of the time the shore is only a short but difficult swim away. I have known more than one patient to drop out of therapy prematurely, rather than deal with personal pain. At first they are willing to share what they feel. Yet when they learn that it is not the therapist who can save them, but only their own choices, they decide that the disease is preferable to the cure. It is hard to watch people make poor, self-destructive choices; but valuing the freedom of others and acknowledging one's own limitations often leaves no other course of action. No one person can choose to grow up for another. And the fact that so few people are willing to face the terror and fear of coming to know who they are does not mean that it is an impossible task which we all ought to be protected from undertaking.

EXISTENTIAL PAIN

There is a third type of pain, which we shall call existential pain. This is the pain of being endowed with an imagination for the possible, which constantly pushes back the horizons of what I desire from the reach of my ability. Existential pain does not arise from my particular experiences, but from my very human existence. It is the pain of realizing that behind the specific physical and emotional pains which confront my desire for pleasure, behind the specific failures which arise from seeking achievements beyond my capacities, behind the specific frustrations of encountering obstacles standing in the way of what I could otherwise do, behind the specific judgments of guilt over behavior inconsistent with my values, and indeed behind every specific experience of my limits—there lie the limits of my very humanity. However I may respond to specific limit-experiences throughout life, there remains to be faced the deep sense of pain of being born into a condition not of my own choosing, of being cursed with a capacity for desire which no specific object can satisfy.

Like physical pain and emotional pain, existential pain is a warning signal of a maladjustment that is begging for correction—except that to correct it would require the ability to re-create my very humanity. It is a sickness of soul which could only be relieved if, like the fisherman's wife in the German fairy tale, I could become God himself. But that choice is obviously not open to me.

On the other hand, just as we would perish biologically without the gift of physical pain, and would arrest the process of growing into insight and intimacy without emotional pain, it may well be that this existential pain has to be seen as the grace of the restless heart that St. Augustine spoke of as having its rest only in God. Rather than viewing the image of God as simply a projection of what man is not but most wants to be, I might then accept it as an image of the final and proper object of all human desire. Rather than serving to *relieve* the pains of my life, the choice to believe in God would *ground* them in a deeper pain, directing my attention to a greater and more encompassing reality transcending the rules and rhythms of man's search for meaning in pain.

SUFFERING AND PAIN

Pain, in the generic sense in which we have used it here, can refer either to a feeling-state that happens to us as a result of spontaneous, irrational processes, or to one that results from deliberate and rational choices. This latter form of pain may be identified specifically as *suffering*. Suffering points to an ineffective way of dealing with pain, whether by denying it or by attempting to anesthetize it. Since the cause of the original pain remains unacknowledged, the pain is bound to reappear in other forms—as suffering. Suffering can be physical, psychological, or existential; and in any of these forms it can serve as a displacement of pain from any other form. Physical discomfort, emotional disturbance, and existential *angst* can then become alarm systems for secondary processes which are all the more easily overlooked, since even if the new signal is acknowledged and its causes sought, one is likely to go looking in the wrong places.

As an example of this displacement of pain, by suffering, from one mode to another, let us look at loneliness. *Loneliness* is a form of emotional pain grounded in the experience of the absence of others. Simply being in the presence of others—even of those whose absence is felt—does not of itself relieve a lonely state, because its causes are emotional. Similarly, reflection on the human condition is an unreliable nostrum for loneliness, since it is a specific loneliness that is causing me pain. Behind the escape from loneliness in the company of friends or crowds lies the decision to interpret my condition as mere physical *aloneness*. Alternatively, behind the escape from loneliness in philosophical or theological mysteries lies the decision to prefer existential *solitude* to the felt absence of other persons. In this way the substitute suffering, while not lessening the pain, may refract my gaze from its primary causes long enough to provide the illusion of relief. Loneliness is the shadow cast by all human intimacy. To deny it is to reject the fullness of the experience of relating and communicating oneself to another person. It may—and probably will—open out into a sense of aloneness and solitude as well; but these ought not be chosen as a defense against an emotional disturbance.

By the same token, loneliness can itself become a pain suffered in order to replace the pains of aloneness or solitude. The physical need for another's company is natural to man as a social animal, and lies at the heart of all sexual expression. It has its own pains and its own warning signals—the feeling of aloneness—which ought to be understood. But if I choose to neglect or fear these impulses, I may find my physical need for another expressed in a mode of emotional pain. Loneliness then becomes an avoidance of causes by a barter of symptoms. The solitude of facing the horizons of our humanity can likewise be transplanted from its existential plane to an emotional pain. In this sense, simplistic academic reductions of religious belief to the pietistic projections of lonely people has the same origins as the pietistic person's refusal to face the felt inadequacy of his religious imagination by transmuting the feelings into a personal longing for the images of belief. Both are choices to prefer loneliness to the actual maladjustment. And, like all suffering, both are ultimately self-defeating.

HELPLESSNESS AND PAIN
When suffering of any sort does not achieve its desired end of lessening pain, it may retire, as a last resort, to a state of deliberate helplessness. If left to run its full course, this state terminates, on the physical plane, in malaise; on the

emotional plane, in depression; and on the existential plane, in alienation. More commonly, our states of helplessness are milder, and as a rule exhibit symptoms of one sort or another on all three planes. In any case, what is essential for helplessness as a condition of suffering, as distinct from a condition of pain due to natural conditions outside our control, is that it *be chosen*. This is essential, because if it can be chosen, it can also be *not* chosen.

At certain times in all of our lives, the condition of helplessness is unavoidable because its causes are determined by the limitations of our very nature. As infants, we would not have survived without someone caring for our needs. At the other end of the spectrum, many of us will live to experience the natural degeneration of old age, when we will rely on others to keep us in their care. Between the extremes of infancy and old age fall other inevitable periods of relative helplessness, depending on our health, on how we take care of ourselves, on accidents, and the like. In each instance, it is our human task accurately to assess just how weak we really are, to accept help when it is realistically needed, and to avoid exacting privileges or taking license. Demanding care from others when we should be caring for ourselves is a demeaning thing in any relationship for both parties involved. But to receive help when it *is* needed and offered is not an insult to our integrity or self-determination. On the contrary, graciously to allow oneself to be cared for in times of incapacitation is among the greatest of our human capacities.

I remember talking over coffee once to a teacher of mine who had some years previously suffered a stroke that left his right side partially paralyzed. He could move about with a cane, but not without considerable difficulty. The conversation turned to physical disabilities and he explained his own feelings this way: "A small incident not too long ago helped me to see how well I am adjusting to this paralysis.

95

When I first had the stroke, my mother visited me and tried to be as helpful as she could. I used to resent her helping me with my coat, or handing me my gloves, or putting on my hat. I knew I could do these things myself, even though it would take a little longer, and I felt infantilized when she did them for me. Then one day, I somehow discovered that I could allow her to do these things without the feeling that she was robbing me of my independence. It was a cold day, and when she put my hat on, she gently tucked my ears in so they wouldn't get cold, and I could accept this without the feeling of resentment, without feeling as though I were a little boy. I realized that, although she was doing the same *thing* she might have done when I was five or six going out into the snow to play, *I* was no longer that little boy. And I could accept her kindness without being threatened. At that moment, I knew that I had taken another step in accepting the situation of helplessness I live with."

This memory stirs another less pleasant one. I recently received a phone call at about four o'clock in the morning. With as much grace as I could muster at that hour, I asked the patient curtly why she was calling me in the middle of the night, what it was she expected me to do, and what her problem was. (I do not muster much grace at four o'clock in the morning.) She replied that she had to see me immediately and could not discuss the problem over the phone. I asked her again what was wrong and why it was so urgent to see me, and she responded, "See, I knew you wouldn't help me," and hung up. She made an appointment a few days later and came to see me. I learned that she had been depressed for over five years, and only had decided during that one sleepless night that it was time to seek help. By hanging up without leaving her name and phone number, she of course made it impossible for me to do anything, even as she blamed me for my inconsiderateness. The choice to be cared for is an important one, but it does not give one the *right* to make the decision of who shall take the care and precisely when.

THE CHOICE IN PAIN

We have been contrasting two modes of responding to pain, of answering the call to alarm on whatever level it reaches us. First, we can react reflexively to the pain itself and disregard its causes. Whether done alone or by entrusting ourselves to another's care, the difficulty with this form of choice in the face of pain is that it is aimed more at retrieving the loss of comfort than at gaining insight into the discomfort; hence the later development of symptoms once-removed from the problem. The second mode of choice in pain is responsibility, i.e., responding as fully as we are able. Again, whether alone or with another's help, the basic structure of the reply is most important: the creative transformation of feelings into behavior in the light of what we value. Choices so made in pain *reflect* the truth of our condition, *correct* what can be corrected and *accept* what we cannot change, and *respect* the desires and limits of others who might take our pain into their care.

The choice not to suffer our pain but fully to experience it bespeaks a reverence for pain as the role it must play in the meaning we give to the things of our life. It acknowledges that besides the ineluctable pains we inherit with our broken humanity, the world is full of pain which it is within our power to eliminate. It expands our sensitivities beyond our skin-bound selves and embraces the community of man in pain. Reverence for pain chooses conflict over comfort, understanding over suffering. For where pain is concerned—with due respect to Aristotle—all of us, every soul of us on earth, desire by nature *not* to know.

97

CHAPTER EIGHT

DEPRESSION

When two animals in the wild are fighting for territorial rights, their contest only rarely ends in death. At some point, one of them capitulates in a gesture of submission, exposing itself defenselessly to the tooth and claw of its victor. The counterpart of this gesture in the human person's battle for responsible self-determination is depression: the choice to submit to forces within or without us judged inimical but too strong for us to cope with. Depression itself is not a feeling that simply "happens" to one. It is a choice, or a series of choices, against continuing to struggle for what we value. It is a self-imposed resignation of responsibility to powers one can neither trust nor control.

Depression affects the entire personality—judgments, imagination, emotions, and physical condition. Because of this, being in the company of a depressed person is exceedingly uncomfortable and frustrating. The demands he makes on others are insatiable because, sadly, the depressed person is usually unaware that his state is a result of his own choices and cannot be relieved simply by allowing himself to be cared for by others. Their attempts to respond only feed his depression by further confirming his submissiveness. And so the circle closes about him slowly, viciously, isolating him without hope or insight.

98

TRAUMATIC DEPRESSION

More important than locating and naming the many symptoms of depression is learning how understanding the roots of depression can help one to overcome it, and how a failure of understanding can condemn one to ever more frequent and more severe periods of depression. To this end, two lengthy excerpts from therapy sessions, which speak for themselves, will make up the substance of my treatment of depression.

The first has to do with a case of deep depression stemming from childhood traumata. Alice, aged thirty-eight, had been happily married for several years when she began to grow increasingly depressed. Over the period of a few years these depressions brought her to the point where she was afraid to leave the house. Her relationship to her husband was good, except that he refused to talk with her about her background in the children's orphanage "because it was too grotesque." When they were no longer able to handle the symptoms of her disturbance, Alice came to see me. The transcript begins with Alice talking about her experiences in the orphanage.

Alice: It was the insecurity of my mother never coming to see me. It was the insecurity of never knowing what to do. It wasn't just one person there telling me what to do, but all of them. You were expected to do things you were never taught to do.

Therapist: Would you say that again?

Alice: What?

Therapist: What you weren't taught but were expected to know.

Alice: Like peeling potatoes. You never had a potato in your hand before, right? But if you gouged out too much of the good part you got your hands slapped and learned not to do it that way. Like ironing. They'd

99

hand you a dress and tell you to iron it. (Beginning to weep slightly) I can remember my sister on this iron mangle. She never worked it before. She got her arm caught in it. It just kept going through.

Therapist: It must have been very frightening to try anything.

Alice (Upset, but trying to control herself): It does become frightening to try it, but you can't do anything about it because you have to do what *they* say. . . . You get frightened to do anything. It's easier to shut down. You don't know what someone's reaction is going to be. There was no comfort. My sister was a year older than I and she was in another dorm. There was only the wall between us, and at night when I used to be afraid I would crawl in bed with her, and if the nun would find us she would rip the covers back . . . (frightened and weeping again) . . . and start whipping both of us with the black belt she wore. And when she did that a couple of times my sister wasn't happy to see me come in any more.

(At this point, Alice began to smile nervously and to laugh slightly. It was obvious that she was trying to restrain her memory of the pain. She paused for a moment, and then broke out in heavy sobbing that left her gulping for air.)

Mary: That's a rotten thing. That's a rotten deal.

Therapist: Yes, it was a rotten deal. It was unfair. But on the other hand, to perpetuate it in your own life, you end up treating yourself rotten and that's worse still. . . . Yes, I think it was a rotten deal. It was a worse background than I have had, and mine has been worse than many of yours here. But when we perpetuate our background in our present lives, that's what's really rotten. A kid has no control in an orphanage. He has no control over his parents, how they treat him. But if

100

we continue to repeat it all in adulthood—that's unfair to ourselves.

(I was not giving the patient a great deal of sympathy here. In fact, I was somewhat angry and allowed this to show. Alice had been getting stuck in the sympathy others were giving her as she told and retold her story, bit by bit, and was getting very little real understanding as a result. I went on, more directly.)

Therapist: You treat yourself as badly as an adult as they treated you as a child in the orphange. You couldn't control it in the past, but it annoys me and angers me to see you continue it in the present, since you do have a choice about how you treat yourself. "Depressed . . . afraid to go anywhere . . . can't move. . ." I don't like it, Alice.

Alice: I think I realize, too, why I am afraid to go anywhere out of the house.

Therapist: You might make a mistake. You might get beaten.

Alice: Yeah. . . . The only times I remember leaving the orphanage before I was adopted was when we were told we were going on a vacation, my sister and I. And at first I didn't realize—I thought it *was* a vacation—that it was really a trial. And if they liked us, they would keep us. But they *never* liked us. One couple did like my sister. I remember I sneezed at the kitchen table and I hadn't covered my mouth with my hand and my sister said to me, "You blew it again." (We had been sent back from another couple and I had blown that too, because they didn't take us to church and I told the sisters by mistake. So when we got back to the orphanage my sister was very angry. She said, "You blew it again.") But this time, *I* really hadn't, because when the case-worker came back she was talking to the woman in the kitchen, who said, "I want to keep Shirley, but I don't want to keep Alice." And the case-worker said, "They can't be separated. You'll have to take them both or you don't take either." So we went back to the orphanage.

Pam: For God's sake, if a woman would get so angry at a child's sneezing, that'd be no place to live! She'd probably beat you up.

Alice: So what? I got beaten up at the orphanage. At least at the house you could have gone outside. You didn't hear bells ringing to go out and bells ringing to come in. There was a yard to walk in. You could walk all over the house. You weren't confined to one place. . . . I wouldn't have had to go back and face that nun I worked with, the one who took care of the children. Getting angry wasn't frightening at that age. It was a comfort.

Pam: How did you show your anger then?

Alice: I mean, it *would* have been a comfort. I don't remember showing anger. I hid it. For years I hid it.

Therapist: Go ahead.

Alice: Well, my sister kept telling me I was goofing it. She was only a year older than I was, but she was the one who told me everything. She was the one who told me we were poor. She was the one who told me to stop waiting at the door for Mom to come visit because she wasn't going to come, and that I was a dumb little kid for just standing there. She was the one that told me, "Now don't blow this one. Do whatever they want. Be really good if you don't want to go back." And I goofed it up. I still can't sneeze, to this day. (Showing how she suppresses a sneeze) And my kids say, "That's silly. What kind of a sneeze is that?"

Therapist: But it's not so silly, is it?

Alice: Maybe not . . . but I can't sneeze. (Begins to cry) Then my job changed in the orphanage. I don't even

102

remember how it happened, but the nun told me I stole a pair of stockings. She said, "I know you've stolen these stockings." And I said, "I didn't." And I hadn't. She lined the young boys up, all seven of them. She pulled my pants down and made me lift up my dress and beat me and she hit me. As she was beating me she was hollering, "This is what happens to people who steal. You will get a beating like this every day until you admit you stole those stockings." I hadn't stolen the stockings. I wouldn't admit it, I don't know why. I wouldn't admit it because I didn't do it. I would go to bed at night and would pray that I would die so I wouldn't have to go back to her. The only way that it ended was one day when we were giving the boys a bath. She couldn't stand to hear the children cry. They were crying, hysterical. She said, "You stop them from crying, and this is how you do it." And she held the boy's head under water. (Alice is practically moaning her words now) When she let him up he was gulping for air, and so she left the room. Then I told them, "Please don't cry. Don't be afraid. Just get in and get wet and come right out, and she won't know that you haven't been washed." But they were too afraid and couldn't stop crying. (Her voice is barely audible now) She came back in and said, "Can't you do anything right? This is how you stop them." And she ducked the boy's head under the water and held it there . . . and he flapped like a seal and he couldn't raise his head . . . And we all cried, "Please let his head up." When he didn't move, she took him out of the tub and carried him away and said, "He won't cry any more." (Long pause) I never saw the boy again. I never saw that nun either. They said they took her away and that the boy was dead.

(At this point there was a vacant stare on Alice's face

and her body was trembling. She looked confused. I had seen this happen before, and each time the group had tried to comfort her and help her *over* her feelings. I decided it was best for her now to try to work *through* them.)

Therapist: Let that cry go, Alice. Don't keep it in. Really *feel* what you feel. Really let it go. (She sobs lightly) Let yourself go.

Alice: Why didn't I do something for him? (Screaming) Why didn't I stop her? (Sobbing louder and louder) Why did I just stand there and just watch her?

Therapist: Let yourself *feel*. Don't ask why—just give yourself permission to feel it.

Alice (Sobbing deeply, wretchedly, loudly, gasping for breath): Why didn't I do *something*?

Therapist: Don't ask yourself why. Just feel it.

(Her cries grew louder and more guttural. Although her entire body was nearly convulsing, I kept encouraging Alice to *feel* her pain, her anger—everything that was inside of her. Many members of the group were weeping along with her. A few sat back in their chairs, petrified at what they were watching. I continued slowly, in a quiet voice, inviting her to feel what was hidden inside of her, without trying to understand it. The crying grew very loud and terrifying, a cry that had been suppressed for over thirty years. Finally she calmed down, and turned to me.)

Alice: How do you get it to go away?

Therapist: You don't. But you don't have to let it torture you.

Alice: Why did I carry this with me all these years? Why didn't I do anything?

Therapist: What could a seven-year-old do?

Alice: (Looking at me, for a few minutes, without words): I feel like an extremely heavy burden has been lifted from my shoulders. I don't understand why I feel so good. I can't ever remember feeling this way.

(I consider it important, after such emotional release, to help the patient gain further insight into what has taken place. Of themselves, feelings are not enough to sustain further choices, though they may help make them possible. I add here only my final summary remark.)

Therapist: When you stop *trying* to make that nun go away, then she *will* go away. When you face the fact that you did what a seven-year-old could do; when you understand how wrong she was, how vicious, and that she should not have treated you that way, then, the pain will stop terrifying you. It's an awful position for a child to be in.

The next morning, Alice reported that she had had the best night's sleep that she had had in years, and was wondering what had happened to her. Other of her depressive symptoms disappeared during the coming weeks, as she began to take positive steps—while still continuing in therapy, for a while—to organize her life more effectively.

ANATOMY OF A DEPRESSION

In Alice's case, depression covered a massive amount of pain which she mistakenly hoped might go away by deciding not to think about it. Her husband unwittingly went along with her poor strategy. Of course, it did *not* go away, and because of that Alice gradually came to hand over the responsibility for her future to the powerful, despairing certainty that what had happened to her once was doomed to repeat itself again. By her choice first to hide her feelings and then to submit to their control over her, Alice had knit herself into an emotional straitjacket that developed into a general state of depression. Although she had been treated badly as a child, she no longer was a child; and yet she clung to the belief that the hurt, the fear, and the guilt which haunted her would surface again and again to destroy her every chance for happiness. Reversal of the depression came about when Alice was willing fully to accept the reality and force of her wounding memories, assess her present situation more objectively, and decide creatively to transform the life that lay ahead of her, rather than erect orphanage walls about every situation she walked into.

The structural anatomy of a depression includes a number of elements, not all of which show up clearly in each instance. Among them are such things as anger, rejection, fear, helplessness, guilt feelings, inadequacy, suffering, and irresponsibility.

Some sense of the depth of anger present in depression can be had by examining how *we* feel when we hear about the people in the orphanage and the parents who rejected little Alice because of an impolite sneeze. The whole sense of unfairness generates feelings of anger in us. But for Alice, her helplessness in the situation precluded expressing anger; she was powerless even to feel what she felt. Regarding her witness of the child's drowning, Alice's fear of doing anything at the time lest it be punished as disobedience, coupled with her anger over the injustice perceived, left her as an adult with feelings of guilt: she condemned herself for not having done something to prevent the senseless death. In this way, the anger of her childhood came to find its expressions finally against herself in the helplessness and guilt feelings of her depression. The process of rejection that had begun in her childhood was complete: she had learned to reject herself and to lay the responsibility for the future on the past.

The depressed person refuses to give up his depression as long as it serves as a possible—even if self-resigning—

expression of feelings of anger, guilt, helplessness, and fear. By insisting that he "can not," rather than "will not," manage for himself, the depressed person manipulates others to make a fuss over him. He demands the attention, but refuses to change. He contributes nothing to his relationships but the story of his discomfort, which he is willing to recount incessantly. He protects himself against the possibility of failure by refusing to choose alternative forms of expressing the feelings he allows to depress him. In terms of a distinction developed in an earlier chapter, the depressed individual *suffers* rather than fully *experiences pain*. For whatever reason he first got involved in hurt, he *stays* there, by choice, to provoke that sympathy of others which he deems essential to survival in the depressed state. All of this was part, too, of Alice's submission to a past she despised but judged beyond her control.

Contracting With Depression

The major therapeutic difficulty in dealing with the depressed person is that he treats his symptoms as the necessary cost of keeping worse things from happening. He welcomes them like hostile companions whose company seems preferable to being left alone. The very emotional warning signals which ought to stimulate change, therefore, are adopted as part of the support system for passive submission.

There is no cure for depression without first letting go of its symptoms and then making an effort to correct the choices that lie behind them. For example, an individual who drinks to relieve his depression is only exchanging one symptom for another. The effects of the "cure" are so short-lived, and its aftereffects so much worse than what it was setting out to alleviate, that the depression can only get worse as a result. Where the process is complicated by addiction, the "cure" becomes at once more appealing, more frequent, and more damaging. Overcoming depression in such circumstances must begin with the choice to stop drinking, in order later to pass on to examining the cause of the depression and correcting it.

In the following verbatim excerpt, we see an example of an individual who had not found sufficient reason to break his contract with depression and preferred its occasional unpleasantness to what he could see as the available alternatives. (Soon after the session on which this recording was made, he discontinued therapy, but continues to suffer from chronic depression.) By way of contrast, we shall meet a woman who was able to conquer severe depression complicated by alcoholic addiction and suicidal tendencies.

The excerpt begins after Frank and Margaret had just successfully resolved some long-standing marital difficulties. I asked the group if anyone wished to respond, and Al was the first to speak.

Al: I think I'd like to say something. I tell you, I wish me and my wife could get stuff like that sorted out.
Therapist: So do I, Al.
Al: I wish my wife were here.
Therapist: How does that make you feel?
Al: Lonely, very lonely. . . . (His attention begins to wander, nervously.)
Therapist: Don't shut down what you feel. I wish your wife were here, too. You've been very brave about going on with your life so far, when she doesn't seem to care at all. You're not alone. Others in the group know what it feels like.
Al: She's out every minute. . . . I don't know what the hell to do. I came out here to see you and felt really fine after the last session. It was one of the few times in my life I could feel with the kids, and with everything, it

was better. But with *her*, if I make the slightest mistake, I get clobbered. . . . Just piddly things. Like last night with her continuous bitching. . . . And then it gets bad with the kids again. You know, like I come home and my oldest son fell off his bike. Okay, he was all bruised and scratched. At first I was mad at him, madder than hell. But I wasn't *really* mad, I guess, I just felt sorry for the kid. He told me what happened. Fine, so it cost me twenty-seven bucks to fix the bike, and I showed him the bill. Well, immediately I come in yesterday and the second one is doing Evel Knievel jumps on his bike. A $127 bike! I was madder than hell, I don't make that kind of money. "Goddammit," I said, "I told you kids not to do that." I went inside and yelled at him and wanted to give him a licking for it and thought to myself, "Dammit, he deserves it, but maybe I'm wrong in doing it. . . ." I don't know, but the thing is, what makes it so hard is, every time I say anything, she says "You come in and yell at us." She mixes in every time I want to say something. If she would once. . . .

Therapist: What's she doing that's *good*?

Al: Huh?

Therapist: What's she doing that's good?

Al: What's *who* doing that's good?

Therapist: Your wife. You were talking about your wife, or weren't you listening?

Al: (Pause . . . Begins to cry)

(During the last session, after which Al said he felt so good, he had done an excessive amount of complaining about his wife. At this point, it seemed important to get him to focus on the more positive parts of his marriage, as a base for change.)

Therapist: It sounds to me very strange that somebody would stay in a situation where he can see all the bad and nothing good.

Al: No, I think she's a good mother. I think she's a good housewife. What makes it hard, Don, is simply that I'm trying my damnedest. I'm scared stiff, you know that, but every time. . . . Like tonight, there's a carpet man working over there. The kids are rambling all over. I can see my wife all excited about it. She says three or four times, "Stop it, stop it, stop it!" So I finally say, "Look. . . ." I mix in. Already I make up my mind I'm going to mix in. I'm scared to mix in, because I want to protect her because she can't get through to the kids. What happens? We had a fight.

Therapist: A "good mother" doesn't need to be protected from her children.

Al: I also think, you know, with my nerves and all besides. . . . I don't know what to do, Don. I just don't know what to do.

Therapist: You seem mad as hell at her, Al.

Al: Yes, damned right I'm mad. (Crying) Sometimes—quite honestly, Don, I've never been this way—but sometimes I could ram my *fist* in her face. Goddammit, she gets me so. . . .

Therapist: Sometimes you could. . . .

Al: God *damn* it!

Therapist: So why do you stay with someone you're so angry at?

Al: Because I love her.

Therapist: What's so lovable about someone you can think so little to say good of?

Al: I don't know. Right now I don't know *what* to say, Don. I really am totally confused. I can't just run out on the situation *all* the time. But I told her. "I don't know how long I can go on with all this." I said, "You always yell at me what I'm doing wrong." Today she told me straight out that there's no one that makes as many bad

110

mistakes as I do. So I said, "Well, heck, that makes you pretty damn stupid to stay with me." I gave her *that* as an answer: "Why the hell are you staying?"

Therapist: Why do *you*?

Al: Huh?

Therapist: Why do *you* stay with *her*?

Al: Because I'm a coward and a chicken and I don't want to lose any more. I've been a loser all my life. I've lost too much already.

Therapist: I believe you.

Al: (Pause. . . . Begins to cry again)

Therapist: (to Ruth): You're nodding, Ruth.

Ruth: Uh huh.

Therapist: Instead of nodding, why don't you talk to Al? I think it might help. It's a situation I'm not faced with, but you are.

Ruth: It's a situation I've been faced with all my married life . . . and I finally did something about it. I went and saw a lawyer a month ago. I'm going to bring it to an end because I can't live like that and he's not going to change. And *I'm* not going to change him. I know, because I've asked and asked him to see somebody for help, but he won't go to *anybody*, because he says he doesn't need help. The problems that he has he'll work out within himself; and *he'll* change, by himself. And I said, "When?" And he said, "Maybe next year, maybe ten years from now, maybe sooner." And that's all. I'm not sitting around waiting, because my life is too short and I see what it's doing to the children. My little girl is so insecure she can't stop crying. Like, she woke up the other night (begins to cry) and said, "Mother, why do I always have such bad dreams?" And because he drinks too. He won't go to A.A. with me. I've asked him, "Try it for ninety days." And he says, "Nope, I can stop any

111

time I want." Hell, I'm not going to sit in that puddle with him. We've been like two kids in a sandbox throwing mud pies back and forth at one another.

Therapist: Ruth, I'm sorry for the pain, but I'm delighted that you are finally facing it and have put your badge of courage on. You were destroying yourself and you have decided not to do that.

Ruth: I'm going through with it. I don't care. I know I'm going to face it. It's going to be—pardon the expression—but when the shit hits the fan, it's going to fly. I know, but I don't care. I really don't. I've had it.

Therapist: If the shit hits the fan and flies, there's less of it to wallow in.

Ruth: That's right. I'm glad I went. The papers haven't been served yet, but I won't sell my life away.

Therapist (to Al): There's *one* response. What's yours?

Al: How the hell does she know what to do with my life? Here I'm sitting with all of this. . . .

Therapist: Make up your mind. *Live* with the pain and with the discomfort or *don't*. But don't live with it and then gripe about it happening.

Al: I'm not ready for it, Don. I can't because the problem thing is, I feel so damn guilty about all of it that it's been told to me all of my life. I've been called so many times a no-good, goddamn sonuvabitch.

Therapist: As long as you choose to believe that there's nothing anybody can do. . . .

Al: Well, the thing is, what *can* you do, Don? It isn't all that easy.

(Note how Al continually backs away from his feelings, by claiming that he is "confused" and "doesn't know," and how by saying he "can't," instead of admitting to himself that he "doesn't want to." Not surprisingly, it is his wife whom he accuses of being unwilling to change.)

Frank: It's not *supposed* to be easy.

Margaret: Yeah, who said it was easy?

Ruth: It's not. I have children. It's not easy.

Al: Well, anyway, why can't they go into *therapy*? They're the ones that belong here. I've told my wife twenty times, "Do me a favor. Please come along."

Ruth: I've tried to talk to my husband about coming, too; but he thinks it's just breaking up our marriage. You're not going to get your wife to come unless she herself decides to.

Al: I was going out to play soccer, and I told her, "I'm not coming home for dinner. I'm coming home, but I'm going right out again at 6:00." And. . . .

Therapist: Wait a minute. I don't care about the bitching and the griping. You may live with it if you want it. I don't and I don't care about your just piling it on all of us here. Tell me what's *good* about your life. I've heard quite enough about what's bad about it—I believe you. But why do you like it that way?

Al: It's true, I do. Then that's what it is. But on the way out here I was thinking about what is good, but frankly, I guess I'm just too goddamn stubborn to throw in the towel yet.

Therapist: All right then, but don't weep when it's your own stubbornness and your own choice. If you don't like it, change it or walk away from it.

Carol: Just a minute ago you said something about feeling "guilty." That triggered something in me: do you maybe feel stubborn because you feel guilty?

Al: No, I don't know *what* this thing is, but what comes out is that I have three children, and they have no other family, and I don't know what's right.

Ruth: I've got three kids, too. And there isn't any "right" way. I always bent over backwards to make people like me, because I felt inferior, and I still have

113

that problem. So I bent over backwards, and I got clobbered every time. When I married my husband, I bent over backwards to make him like me and to make his mother like me. I did everything they wanted and got clobbered right down the line. So I began to blame *them* for everything, until I realized they were just intimidating me because I liked it. But it was *me. I* felt worthless. *I* had to think well of myself before they could be expected to change. I was hiding behind alcohol and the problem just kept getting bigger and bigger, and the alcohol got worse and worse. So Don told me to stop drinking. That's not easy to do; but once I did, I started looking inside. What I had to work on was still there, in me, but I felt confident. I had to grow up as a person. I began to get stronger and to see that I didn't need the alcohol. And I can see how frightened my husband is now. He's scared to death, sitting there looking at me. And there I am, open and honest with him. I answer him right out now. I told him, "I don't like living like this. I'm miserable. I rejected you completely as a man, as a husband. I don't love you. Do you enjoy living like this?" And his answer was, "You're always miserable." Maybe three years ago he would have been right, and it would have made me feel bad. But it doesn't any more. It just makes me feel he has opened the door wider and helped me get out faster. But he's a frightened man, and I feel sorry for him. I really do, because unless he looks at himself and starts to work with himself. . . . He's angry as hell at his mother for doing what she's doing to him, and what she's done. He's angry at the world. He's suffered an awful lot of pain, and I'm only perpetuating the situation by staying there, because he'll never get better just by *my* wanting it. It only gets worse, because I give him

114

an easy way out. And all the times, we're fighting like cats and dogs. He's happy to sit in his little puddle because I'm his mother, taking care of him. And when I leave, he's going to be the saddest person on earth.

Therapist: I think that's just about as neat a summary as I've heard of someone who has in effect said: "I threw the responsibility and control of my life onto others whom I couldn't trust and didn't love. I've now taken it over for myself. I am not only going to take responsibility for what I do from here on in, but for the way things turned out as they did. I gave them power over me. And as long as I did that, I perpetuated it."

(To Al) And if *you* can face these facts in your life, that in some way *you* are responsible for it, then you can change. I know I couldn't have said it more clearly. Ruth was in much worse shape than you. Much worse. My first concerns for her, and we talked about these before, were how I could keep her from running out to commit suicide, how I could stop her from becoming a confirmed drunkard, how I could stop her from hurting someone in one of her states. And those were just the openers. (To Ruth) I think you're fantastic.

Al: Yeah, you've gone through a lot.

Ruth: I let alcohol almost stamp me out.

Al: When I listen to it, I have to admit, that it scares the hell out of me.

Ruth: It scared the hell out of me, too. I've known loneliness. I've known abandonment. I've known the feeling that there is nothing else if I give up what I've got.

Therapist: But what Ruth discovered was—herself. And you, Al, you give your wife enormous power over you. You fight for the control with her, but don't really want it. . . . I don't know if there's anything more that the rest of us can say at this point. Unless you want to say something.

Al: No. I think I know what I have to do.

It seems that what Al knew he had to do was to give up the group. Some members of the group did not so easily give up on Al. Yet when they called on him, his only reply was, "It can't help. I only make things worse between my wife and me by thinking about it." Ruth's divorce went through and she is doing well. While divorce was a reasonable solution *for her*, it probably is not for Al. But the very *thought* of alternatives terrified him, because he preferred to walk stooped over and depressed to standing erect and responsible.

CHAPTER NINE

SEXUALITY

It will hardly have escaped the reader's notice through the course of these chapters that my classifications of valuing, feeling, understanding, imagining, and of psychic behavior in general have proved in each instance somewhat arbitrary. This is always and of necessity the case, as clinical experience confirms again and again. The unfathomable mystery of the human personality stands in perpetual protest against each typology we devise to explain its nature and processes. And it ensures that no sooner do we set out abstemiously to follow a single thread than we are fast led astray in the fascinating weave of interlacing patterns.

Perhaps no aspect of the mystery of man exposes the weaknesses of a psychological system so clearly as sexuality. It is the limit-experience in which everything that is unknown and uncontrollable about human life finds its clearest expression and convergence. But for that very reason, no one who values living by choice can fail to wrestle with the ecstasy and the enchantment, the pain and the helplessness, the ideas and the images, the fear, the anger, and the guilt that come together in human sexuality. Only by restricting sexuality to certain of its elements can we capture it in tidy categories of meaning. Left on its own, it remains a permanent challenge to our goal of self-determination. In this sense, the modern tendency to convert sexual experi-

117

ence into a commodity for consumption —making it dependent solely on the availability and manipulative techniques of a competitive market—is a choice against its fullness and inexhaustible intelligibility.

SEXUALITY AND WHOLENESS

The prevalent bias that "anything goes" in sexuality, or that "whatever takes place between two consenting adults is beyond reproach," is a direct denial of any possible intrinsic relationship between sexual behavior and the traditional values of intimacy and fidelity. It is precisely this bias that I wish to argue against in what follows. I shall assume the position that anything does *not* go in responsible sexual expression, that a mere contract of consent between adults does *not* guarantee that what happens sexually between them is wholesome. Wholesome—the very word sounds Victorian to our ears. But I know of no other that so well describes the meaning of human sexuality. Sex should *tend to wholeness*. It should involve the whole person and promote the whole person, so that he or she feels more together, more integrated, more complete as a result of the chosen expression of sexuality; so that each person expressing himself sexually to another feels more whole in the relationship, in the communion.

So much of sexuality is just the opposite. It fragments, it divides, it isolates. Excessive concern with the physiological aspects of sexual functioning severs a person from himself, making the rest of him in effect a mere appendage to the genital organs. The unabashed Playboy philosophy makes sex a toy, a plaything divorced from personal and emotional expression except insofar as these serve to heighten pleasure. So deprived of its full context, sexuality widens the rift between persons, rather than narrowing it by the choice for mutual commitment. Sexuality turned in on itself becomes

118

masturbation—whether alone or under the pretense of participation—and as a result, an activity otherwise capable of expressing intimacy only isolates.

It is the tension between the capacity of sexuality on the one hand to be a sign of the deepest fidelity and communication, and on the other to be trivial, commonplace, and selfish, that marks human sexuality as distinct from animal behavior. The fact that sexuality is at once able to express the loftiest and the lowliest of human sentiments makes it a continual challenge to responsible human living. It is essentially and irrevocably ambiguous: however trivial, its nobler possibilities cannot entirely be erased and somehow always manage to surface; and however noble, the traces of triviality and self-preoccupation are never wholly absent.

THE LIMITS OF SEXUALITY

Like pain, failure, frustration, and guilt, sexuality confronts us with the experience of our human limits. The desire for a self-transcendence that is not self-destructive, for a full union with another that does not forfeit the individuality of either, finds its greatest expectations in sexual desire, but is doomed ultimately to remain unsatisfied. The illusion of fully participated and mutual care may be created between two persons for a fleeting moment of passion, but it must finally dissipate as they fall out of one another's arms. The intimacy which we seek is not within our power to achieve. Only by denying care for the other, or for oneself, can one sustain the belief that sexual expression has been fulfilling, that the limit has been conquered.

Earlier we saw how simple *reaction* to limit-experiences by hiding is an abuse of self-determination: a choice *not* to choose. The same is true in sexuality. When a person attempts to deny the imagined desire for intimacy, fidelity, and communion, his sexuality becomes perverted, brutal,

119

careless. Alternatively, by denying that sexuality is always in part trivial and selfish, a person trims his desires down to the size of his own inflated altruism. This latter frequently masquerades as the spiritualization of love, only to avoid acknowledging the devaluation of physical desire as evil, dirty, or bestial.

Humor is another form of reactionary response to sexual limits. Much of the appeal of sexual jokes is that they tease us into recalling the incongruities of our sexuality. The play of a good sexual joke usually involves a clever mixture of the lofty and the low parts of sexual experience. The indiscriminate rejection of all such humor as base ignores the inevitable baseness in all sexual behavior; just as the exclusive dependence on such humor for one's meanings ignores the sublimity of all sexual behavior.

Responsibility for sexual limits begins with *accepting* those limits. Acceptance is obviously not the same as toleration. A person who is willing to tolerate sex in order to keep his mate, or who engages in sexual activity only to relieve physical tension, is hardly behaving responsibly. Acceptance means acknowledging the fullness of sexual desire and expression for what it can do—offer a pleasurable opportunity for increasing intimacy, fidelity, and communion—and for what it *cannot* do—bring total mutual care free of all selfishness and triviality.

Responsibility for our sexuality is completed in the *creative transformation* of its limits. Love, care, and affection are the transforming virtues of sexuality. Sexual expression both celebrates and creates its desired intimacy. Sexuality with commitment and fidelity establishes a relationship of mutual re-creation, and can be pro-creative of children. None of the other limit-experiences is as intrinsically related to creative transformation as is human sexuality.

Some of the implications of this position need further

development, and will occupy the attention of the rest of this chapter.

Modes Of Irresponsibility

Irresponsible sexuality, we have said, is sexual behavior that is not wholesome and does not foster integrity, but rather divides or isolates. It loses sight of either the nobility or the triviality of sexuality, and so denies its limits. Working from this model, we may single out a number of the modes of irresponsible sexual activity.

Masturbation is trivial sex. Of itself it is not horrible, evil, or perverse. It is simply trivial—pleasant enough, but devoid of human communication. As sexuality becomes an expression of behavior with interpersonal significance, problems of masturbation generally decrease. That sex is *sometimes* trivial is no cause for alarm; that it is *primarily* trivial is an indication that the full human context of sexuality is missing. In adolescence, before sexuality has been integrated into the personality through relationships with some commitment and sharing, masturbation may be the method for release of sexual tension. It becomes problematic, however, when it inhibits the adolescent from seeking adequate relationships, when he makes a habit of it for the sheer pleasure of it, or when he tries to make masturbation something other than trivial sex, like a terrible disease to be cured at all costs or an expression of character weakness to be brought under control.

Masturbation, as trivial sex, is not necessarily done alone. Much of sexuality in marriages, for example, where commitment and fidelity are lacking, has to be seen as mutual masturbation.

When an individual loses sight of the fullness of human sexuality, he may become promiscuous. For many, of

121

course, this is not a question of *losing* sight of the goal but of never having *had* it in the first place, of lacking any positive experience of personal intimacy. This is often the case among young people who see no alternative to their promiscuous activities. (The same often holds true for the prostitute whose promiscuity is chosen for other motives, and in whose case the perversion of sexuality is often complicated by symptoms of frigidity.)

It has long been clear to me that sex is a good technique for getting people close enough to begin talking about what really matters to them. By drawing people out of their privacy and bringing them physically near, sexual activity can encourage deep emotional and intellectual sharing as well. But physical proximity can also be an effective way of avoiding participation in truthfulness and affection. It can substitute as a form of expression for other feelings, too— like fear and anger, for instance. A person afraid of homosexuality may act out heterosexually in order to dispel his fears about his sociosexual identity. An individual who is angry may release his anger in sexual exploits and conquests, in violent or nonviolent rape. A woman may become frigid when angry at her husband. A man may become sexually brutish when fearful of his virility. It becomes important, therefore, to discern in each instance what is really being expressed in sexual behavior. Two lonely, frightened adolescents clinging to each other in bed might better begin to deepen the intimacy they seek by admitting the fear and anger that drove them together for mutual protection and security.

Adolescence is a time for learning about full human relationships and for experimenting with intimacy. Sexuality takes an abrupt and commanding importance in this process all too soon. Sexual relations are frequently viewed as the only testing ground for the stability of commitments in relationships of love and care. Yet premature sexual expression can effectively *remove* the risk of a relationship rather than *clarify* it, and often does precisely that.

I remember one young lady who took the view that her relationship with her boyfriend, with whom she was living, was really a kind of "trial marriage." "We share everything and are committed to each other," she exclaimed, "so why shouldn't we sleep together as well?" I pointed out that I was suspicious of their commitment and suggested that the security she had found was blinding her to the facts. She rejected the idea out of hand. "What kind of car does your boyfriend drive?" I asked. "Oh, he's got a new Corvette," she announced proudly. "Good," I replied, "since you share *everything*, why not ask him to put the car in your name as well as his own?" "He'd do it in a minute," she insisted. "And just to prove you're wrong, I'll ask him." When she did, her companion snapped at her, "What, do you think I'm crazy? That car costs *money*." The girl learned the hard way that she was worth sharing sex with him, but not worth sharing things that cost money.

One cannot generalize from such examples, of course. And I myself have met couples living together outside of marriage who seem to be building successful, mature relationships as a result of their decision. But in my experience, this is the exception. More often than not, one or the other party gets hurt badly by the disillusionment of eventual rejection. If sexual pleasure is viewed as a commodity, a pastime to be arranged whenever possible, or if it no longer has marriage as its primary referent, then the presumption must be that "anything goes" between consenting adults. But if the traditional values of commitment, fidelity, and mutual care are seen as more important than the consumption of pleasures, and if marriage is still accepted as the basic cultural unit of the society we live in, then the burden of disproving irresponsibility seems to me to fall on premarital sex.

123

The irresponsibility of so-called liberated sex is that it is truncated. In disposing of the conventional inhibitions against sexual expression, sex usually ends up divorced from a shared life as well. The sexual ethic of former generations left a great many people with guilt-ridden, unsatisfying sex lives; where there was a shared life, sexuality was often not a wholesome part of it. Now, on the other hand, the uninhibited expression of sex has the opposite result: a sexual relationship with little shared life. A committed relationship is more likely to lead to satisfying sexual relations than a pleasant sexual contract is apt to lead to commitment. Both relationships are incomplete, but sexuality liberated from commitment seems more irresponsible.

Extramarital "affairs" belong to this mode of irresponsibility. Consider a married man and a married woman, both having trouble with their spouses but finding one another sexually compatible. Should they decide to get involved under such circumstances, it is likely they will only end up with an extra unhappy and dishonest relationship to contend with. The life they share with their spouses, which is endangered by internal difficulties, will be further complicated by their external sexual involvement, and hence less likely to reach a satisfactory resolution. Here again, the irresponsibilities are so many and so patent that it is a rare instance that an affair—secret or open—can be helpful in sorting out marital problems and making responsible choices about them.

HOMOSEXUALITY

Homosexuality is, to my thinking, a truncated relationship. It is irresponsible to the extent that the limits imposed by the relationship make impossible the specifically human values of mutuality, commitment, fidelity and communion. It is not a disease, but an incomplete form of relationship.

124

In other words, I think that the possibility of growth in care through sexuality is greater in a heterosexual context than in a homosexual one. A mature person would not prefer someone of his or her own sex unless external circumstances made heterosexual relationships impossible or extremely difficult.

Homosexuality is chosen as a way of life by default, not simply as an alternative to available heterosexual relationships. There may be explanations in terms of personal experience which make the choice intelligible, and I do not wish to stand in judgment over those who have made such choices. But I do stand by the view that homosexuality as a way of life is chosen by default, and that as a way of life it puts important limits on the expression of properly human values.

People choose a homosexual way of life for a wide variety of reasons. A person who has been intimidated or otherwise driven to a low level of self-esteem may cling to his own sex for protection. Relations with the opposite sex may make too many demands on such a person. Homosexuality seems to attract people who fear intimacy and yet cannot cope with loneliness. It offers a refuge for hatred, anger, and fear of competition. Moreover, I can say, on the basis of my practice, that I have never met a person preferring homosexuality who did not have a disturbed childhood. Nor have I seen a child raised by caring, open, and honest parents who preferred homosexuality to heterosexuality in adulthood.

It seems true that there is a greater proportion of fairly healthy, stable homosexual women than men. This may have something to do with current cultural biases. Two women can live together and express their intimacy much more openly and without fear of inflaming continual suspicion and outraging the conventional conscience than can two men.

125

Of all the homosexuals (male and female) I have treated, there has not been a single case in which a patient has not changed his sexual orientation as a result of therapy. Some did drop out of treatment because they claimed they preferred not to change, but they recognized in each case that it was a question of choice, not impossibility.

I realize that much of what I have had to say in this chapter regarding premarital sex, extramarital sex, and homosexuality runs counter to prevalent attitudes. I too am seeking clarification in the maze of opinion and data that exists, even as I try to be consequential with my basic values. As I learn more about human functioning and behavior, my position may change again, as it often has in the past. What I have offered here is simply my best estimates of how sexuality can be expressed in a caring, responsible, self-determinative fashion. I feel rather more confident of the basic structure of the argument, and more uncertain of its specific application. But uncertainty is nothing new to me. Indeed, the mysteries of the human personality that unfold before me in my life and practice have almost made it a way of life.

CHAPTER TEN

THERAPY

People do not usually go to see a psychotherapist simply because they are in *pain*. They go because they suspect their pain is a *suffering* of their own choosing which counsel and understanding can help correct. I rarely see a patient—the word means "one who suffers"—who does not already have a good intuitive grasp of the decisions he needs to make in order to reverse his pattern of mental or physical discomfort. Unfortunately, patients do not often trust their own suspicions as much as they fear the psychologist's "magical art" of seeing right through people. And so a good deal of time is spent sorting out their own deeper intuitions from the incredibly intricate stories they invent to protect their innocence and deny their complicity in the state of affairs that led them to me in the first place. Once that is done, therapy can begin.

PRINCIPLES

Psychotherapy is a moral enterprise through and through. As the Greek word *therapeia* suggests, it is a service rendered to the temple gods: to the values which we house in judgment, which we consult in decision, and whose bidding we specify in behavior.

The clinical setting of psychotherapy is a kind of microcosm in which the patient can reconstruct the macrocosm of

127

his life, examine it critically, and attempt to discern the cause of his suffering. It achieves its purpose when it has brought about a conversion, a shift of perspective. It does not offer asylum from the tribulations of life, but a new way of viewing them: as a challenge rather than as a threat. The therapist's job is to facilitate the transferral of responsibility for maladjustment to the only therapist who can effect lasting change—the patient himself. It is for this reason that I choose to refer to my theory and practice as the psychology of self-determination.

The success of the psychotherapeutic encounter depends, in large part, on both the skills and the integrity of the therapist. Professional incompetence is, obviously, irresponsible and risky. But professional competence can never be enough. If the therapist is perceived as honest, frank, and caring, the patient is more apt to put a premium on the same virtues in dealing with his own life. If the therapist is perceived as curious, antagonistic, distant, or secretive, the patient will probably only decrease in self-esteem and become more deeply entrenched in the routine of poor choices that lie behind his suffering. The only protection the therapist has against encouraging such things is to have his own life in order.

Most of the specific principles which ground my therapeutic practice have been expounded at one point or another in the course of the previous chapters. I need only repeat them briefly here. My basic assumption is that maladaptive behavior is learned, goal-oriented, and value-laden. Accordingly, effective change entails learning a new set of values—or, more frequently, reaffirming certain neglected values—and embodying them in concrete goals, then adapting behavior to meet those goals. Each step of the process involves choice. Symptomatic behavior—choosing to suffer or hide from a conflict situation—and fully responsible behavior—choosing to accept and creatively

128

transform a situation—are both forms of self-determination and hence the object of therapeutic concern. The images, feelings, and limit-experiences themselves, which are constellated spontaneously, are not a matter of choice but form the context within which the therapy must take place.

I assume that people who come to see me are coming with a value system somewhat different from my own, and with a different set of presumptions about the nature of therapy. I usually try to clarify my theoretical position, therefore, at the very first interview, in order that the patient is free to choose to continue or to terminate before fundamental differences are allowed to interfere with the therapeutic process. In many cases, the patient acknowledges such differences but chooses to proceed nonetheless, precisely in order further to investigate them.

Moreover, it is material at the outset to discuss, at least in a general way, what each party expects from the other and from the therapeutic encounter. The terms of such a "contract" are always negotiable as therapy progresses, of course, but I consider it important not to risk deceiving my patients or to presume too readily that they know what they are getting into.

At times, especially with children, preliminary discussion of theory and methods must be temporarily waived until treatment has begun. The idea of entrusting their emotional lives to a stranger is hardly one children naturally relish or would themselves choose in the first place. However much the basic ground rules can be handled with the parents or guardians of the child, in time his own judgment must be consulted and respected. And if the child is genuinely uninterested in changing or receiving therapeutic direction of any kind, then trying to change him— "convince him to be better" is the euphemism I am usually given—would be an irreverent and short-sighted procedure. In a similar vein, the patient who comes to inform me of his spouse's or child's or brother's or friend's problems cannot be confronted with questions of "contract" until he is willing to admit that it is *he* who wants to change. If this is denied often and firmly, I feel I have no choice but to believe him and dismiss him from treatment on the grounds that therapy cannot take place by proxy. Even where I am relatively certain that he is hiding from himself by projecting his conflicts onto others, to "trick" him into confession would be prying of the sort I find incompatible with care for a patient. Finally, and most difficult of all, are referrals from courts or schools where the one responsible for the patient has no interest in my basic assumptions but is only concerned with correcting maladjusted behavior patterns in the most effective way possible. Here too I generally see such people only once or twice unless they themselves choose to return. I try to make it clear to them that their reasons for *coming* to see me need not be their reasons for *staying*. If an individual wants to change, he will easily overcome his resistance to being coerced into seeking help. If he does not, I do not attempt to coerce him further.

INDIVIDUAL THERAPY

Let us say a patient admits his suffering—and the great majority fall into this category from the very beginning— and is willing to contract with me in order to seek out a creative response to it. I will then administer a battery of tests, the number and nature to be determined by the first interview. (Among those I most often use are the Thematic Apperception Test, the Sentence-Completion Test, the Minnesota Multiphasic Personality Inventory, and the 16 Personality-Factor Test.) My purpose in using these tests is to help discern the actual values operating in a person's life. I make clear to the patient that such testing is useful only as a preliminary indicator, as a way of providing a set of questions to be examined, and not as a "diagnosis" of an "illness" in order to prepare a program for "curing" it.

I also ask the patient to write a personal history in answer to the question "What have I been doing with my life?" Some refuse; most resist at first, claiming that there is not much to write about or that their memory is poor; some few produce massive accounts full of senseless trivia. But when the project is taken seriously, it proves extraordinarily helpful. Not only does it collect a good deal of data, but it also provides a look at the specific structures with which an individual organizes his past, and so brings to light acquired patterns of responding to situations emotionally and intellectively. Most patients are not accustomed to thinking about their past as a whole, but quickly discover that releasing memory spawns other memories long forgotten, and so sets up a broader context for their present suffering.

I seldom read the patient's life history until *after* interpreting the test material with him, although it is completed before this. The usual outcome of these preliminary procedures is the patient's awareness of the accuracy of the tests and of his own intuitive capacity for locating the sources of his problems, a capacity that will eventually enable him to seek ways of resolving them responsibly. It also helps remove the temptation, on my part, of trying to adjust the test results to the personal history.

The major disadvantage to the life history is that it gives encouragement to those who delight in telling and retelling their tales of woe. Depressed patients particularly enjoy recounting their sorrows. The psychosomatically ill have endless medical histories ready for the willing listener. Delinquents easily get distracted in relating episode after episode of their run-ins with the law. Indeed, at some point nearly every patient turns to the past as the safest and most available strategy for escaping the present.

As stated at the conclusion of the chapter on "beginnings," the psychotherapist's concern with the past is for the insight it can bring to the present moment. When there is danger of addiction to the stories of things past, I try to direct attention to the patient's failure to change, to his actual suffering. By confronting him with his retreat into memory as a form of hiding, the focus can shift to the programming of intellectual and emotional responses as a detriment to self-determination. Throughout, I struggle not to hide my own feelings and judgments from my patients. Whether I feel angry, sad, affectionate, or frightened, I share this with them immediately; in the same way I let them know at each step my understanding of what they are doing and why they are doing it.

Inertia in the face of a perceived need to change is often protected by a transference of the responsibility from the past to the insurmountable obstacles of the present. Almost inevitably, the therapist ends up taking the blame for the patient's failure to change. I remember a sixteen-year-old student who was referred to me by the police for stealing, truancy, and trafficking in drugs. He showed a real desire to change and seemed to be doing well for a few months, when he abruptly decided to stop therapy. He told me that his mother was complaining about my bill. I accepted the possibility that the expense may have become a burden to his parents, and so agreed to see him without fee for three months. Shortly thereafter he announced that his father was complaining about having to drive him to and from my office. I offered to try to make some other arrangement for transportation. A week later he got his driver's license and terminated therapy, claiming that I wasn't helping him any more. His behavior had improved and he continued to keep out of trouble with the police. But he had not achieved everything he had hoped for. His mother, his father, and finally I were all blamed for not doing what only he could do.

In general, a patient who wants to change but does not want to assume the discipline of concrete choices will recover equilibrium by blaming the "force of circumstances"; by accusing the therapist of incompetence and lack of care; or by becoming excessively preoccupied with some personal weakness or other of the therapist's that he has been able to discover in the course of their encounters. There are instances, of course, where the therapist *can* be inhibiting the patient's progress and blaming the patient. This is the greatest risk of the therapeutic encounter, and can only be minimized by the concerted and unrelenting effort to examine one's own honesty when confronted with such accusations. There are also cases in which external circumstances *do* stand in the way. Wherever possible, I invite the significant parties to meet with the patient. If this is not possible, the treatment has to proceed with insufficient data and some way has to be found of assessing and correcting the interference.

GROUP THERAPY

Once having taken a serious look at his past and adequately having assessed his present situation, it is natural for the patient's attention to turn towards the future. Many of the obstacles which block this shift of perspective, such as those discussed above, become more apparent and are more quickly laid aside in a group setting. Hence I encourage those who are open to the idea to participate in a long "Self-Determination Session." (Where an individual is so frightened or disturbed or insecure that group work would be counterproductive, I continue with him in individual therapy.) Group process focuses an individual's problems in a way that the therapist-patient setting often cannot. The patient is more easily able to see that his tendency to blame past or present circumstances for his paralytic posture towards the future is in fact ambivalent. On the one hand, it is protective of the status quo and thus, irresponsible; on the other, it points to the need for the support and care of others, and the fear of isolating oneself by responsible decisions. The group cannot change actual external conditions past or present, but it can provide a social setting in which the individual can experiment with and diminish the anxiety of assuming new and more responsible roles in his outside life.

The same principles that govern individual therapy remain in force in the group setting, and the patient is given to understand that it may be necessary to disclose and reexamine things handled previously only in our private encounter. For that reason, I expect of each member of the group the same commitment of confidentiality that I make to them severally.

The initial long Self-Determination Session is conducted with from eight to fourteen participants and runs from three to four days. During that time the group lives together and determines its own best rhythm of work, sleep, and eating. One month later there is a follow-up gathering, generally lasting only a few hours. The purpose of this meeting is to evaluate the long session and to determine a course of action thereafter. Some members decide to terminate therapy at that point, and for many of them it is a natural and healthy step. I suggest to most, however, that they continue minimally by attending a two-hour monthly meeting for approximately six months. Only rarely does it seem appropriate to return to individual therapy.

As a complement to individual therapy, the long session, follow-up meetings, and monthly get-togethers are all

134

aimed at helping the individual to further discover the healing power of imagining, feeling, understanding, and choosing, and of entrusting his suffering to the care of other concerned individuals. To this end, the group process allows certain procedures and techniques not possible in the individual encounter, or at least not capable of the same impact. Several of these have appeared in the verbatim extracts scattered throughout this book. I should like to offer here one final example, in order to illustrate the way in which therapy can be enhanced by "corrective experiences" in group therapy.

Sister Grace was a thirty-two-year-old Roman Catholic nun. She was becoming increasingly restless and discontent with her religious life, and came to see me for treatment. Her life history revealed how, in her early teens, her father had thrown her onto a haystack and raped her. She bore the scars on her arm where a pitchfork had pierced her as a permanent reminder. As she later discovered, joining the celibate life was her way of protecting herself from the sexual onslaughts of men, for she had come to believe, on the basis of her traumatic experience as a child, that all men were sexually brutal. The fear had spread to other areas of her life, and she was finding herself increasingly cynical, distant, and distrustful. At the same time she was a rather seductive person, and this disturbed her. She would engage men often and at great lengths in intellectual, academic discussions on topics which interested her little or not at all—simply in order to get the attention she wanted and yet feared. She decided to take part in a group session.

When her turn came to speak, she explained her situation to the others in the group in a cold, devil-may-care tone. She sounded like a tired social worker expounding on someone else's background, without feeling and without any apparent determination to change. The group was getting nowhere with their protests. I asked Grace if she was really interested in changing the direction of her life. "Of course," she said, "that's why I'm here." I then asked her to remove her clothes. She objected, clutching her arms tightly about her shoulders: "Isn't there any other way? Can't we just *talk* about this?" "We could, Sister," I replied. "But you have been talking about this to us for *three days*, and to other therapists for *three years*. Do you want to face your problem or not?" "I'm not going to take my clothes off for anyone," she insisted. I retreated from her decision, telling her that there might be other ways of helping her discover her feelings, that she was the one most likely to discover the right means, and that I would respect her choice. She calmed down and remained silent for several minutes. "Okay," she said, breaking the silence, "if that's what it takes, I'll drop my clothes." I assured her again that it was not necessary, that it was her own choice. She stood up and disrobed, and I did the same. I stood in front of her. "Sister, not every man is a rapist. Not every man will hurt you or ridicule you. Do you think I care so little for you?" Her body stiffened, her eyes glazed, and then in almost convulsive fashion she threw her arms about me and began to weep uncontrollably. Years of bitter pain were being released. The terror that had been her constant companion since childhood had come out at long last. The situation had recalled her childhood trauma, as she knew it would, but had corrected it by removing the fear and the hurt. I did not take advantage of her or humiliate her; but neither did I confirm her conviction that the body was something evil or dangerous. The rest of the group was extremely supportive and understanding. Several months afterwards, Grace left religious life and about a year later married, and is now the mother of a delightful little baby boy. The life she had wanted but feared to choose is hers at last to face with courage and responsibility.

Psychotherapy is not a wonder drug or a parlor game. It's

dangerous in the hands of the unprepared. Psychotherapy is a slow learning process in which the patient comes to sort out his values and the service rendered to them in his goals and choices. It is not the privilege of the therapist to expect of his patient anything he is unwilling to engage in himself. Nor is it his role to stand in moral judgment over his patient, but to help him uncover the morality inherent in his suffering. In short, psychotherapy is the art and theory of promoting the possibility and desirability of responsible self-determination.

EPILOGUE

Last summer I did something I had talked about for years: I spent a week alone in the woods. I brought no food or tobacco or coffee or alcohol. I left behind my books and writing materials, my radio and my tape recorder. The only reminders of civilization I allowed myself were a great jug of purified water, a tent, a can of insect repellent, a pair of hiking boots and a few clothes.

So equipped, I arrived early one morning at the monastery in whose 3,000 acres of woods the local abbot had kindly agreed to let me "make myself at home." He even offered to ask one of the monks to check up on me daily—a standard procedure, I was later to learn, for any of their number who felt inclined, as I did, for a longer time apart. I agreed, and Father Dominic was assigned to drive me out to the edge of the farmland, which was as far as their small truck could make it. The pair of us then set out along a small stream that wound its way deeper and deeper into the forest. Some two miles later we arrived at a high, level spot opening out onto a magnificent view of the valley below. There we pitched the tent. "How do you feel?" asked Father Dominic. "Excited," I replied. "You will have felt a good deal more than that by the time you leave here," he told me, smiling, and departed.

For the first few hours I was certain he had been mistaken. Nestled up there among the trees and hills, I was

138

quite overwhelmed by the colors and smells and sounds of my new neighborhood. It seemed as if I had never breathed fresh air before, as if I were feeling the warmth of sunshine for the very first time. I took off my clothes and began to wander, content and alone.

Slowly my excitement wore off and, as dusk began to settle on the woods, turned to fear. I might have hidden behind the facts of the situation—for I was really quite safe—but had decided I would let my feelings guide me in my solitude. My fear grew, and soon there was no turning back. I was terrified. No one to turn to, no cigarettes to reach for, no bottle of Scotch to calm me, nothing. Every noise in the bushes became a great wild beast stalking me (even though Father Dominic had assured me that the most ferocious thing I was likely to encounter was a stray cow). Every rustle of the wind was the start of a hurricane (although I was hundreds of miles from the sea). Every flutter of wings was an anxious vulture waiting to pick my bones clean, if the other predators didn't carry them away to some secret cave where I would never be found. There was no escape from my imagination. I curled up inside my tent, quivering, and cried myself to sleep.

I think I have never felt, before or since, the blessing of a sunrise as much as I did when dawn finally arrived the next morning. I had survived the night. But soon things got worse. By ten o'clock the heat had become oppressive and I was convinced the trip had been a great mistake. I had never really known why I set out on the expedition in the first place, I reasoned, so perhaps the best thing would be to turn back. Lonely, depressed, and longing for comfort, I picked up the only literature at my disposal: the label on my can of insecticide. And there I read, in bold red letters: WARNING! CONTENTS UNDER PRESSURE. So there it was, in four short words, my problem. I was retreating from the heat, seeking refuge in a cool, dark place in order to avoid the explosion of images, feelings and questions I feared would be too much for me to manage. As I walked about, calmer but still aghast at the discovery, Father Dominic suddenly appeared. "I see the excitement has gone," he began. "What are you going to do now? There *is more*, you know, if you choose to stay." If you choose to stay—the phrase seemed to linger like smoke in the air. If I choose to stay. I did not have to be there; I could leave. But I could also stay, if I chose to. I asked Father Dominic to come back in two days.

Once I realized that *I* had determined to remain, the fear vanished and was replaced by a curious peacefulness that never left me for the rest of my time there. I got down to the business of being alone in the woods. For hours I watched, and listened. I began to see myself as an intruder, a trespasser on foreign soil, there among the shrubbery and the trees, the flora and the animals. And I hoped they would not treat me in their home the way I would treat most of them in mine.

I soon learned that I had pitched camp close to a den of muskrats, who would occasionally poke their heads out from behind a bush. If I moved at all, they would scamper off. If I kept still, one or the other would venture close to me, within arm's reach. And so it was I sat for long periods quiet and motionless, hoping to woo their return—I could not say how long; I had not brought a wristwatch. During that time I learned a lot about waiting, about "letting go" of the urge for immediate satisfaction so bred into us by consumer propaganda. I also began to appreciate afresh that this very ability to wait and to think would keep me permanently distant from the muskrats, however successful I might be in drawing them near. They seemed to be free. They could go where they wanted, sleep whenever they wished, limited only by their physical instincts. But I could *choose* to be there, and they could not. I could *reflect* on the laws of my nature, and they could only *obey* theirs.

The next day, while hiking about in search of adventure, I got lost. I knew that there were farmhouses a few miles away and could see them from time to time through a break in the trees on the ridges. But a naked hitch-hiker with heavy army boots and a can of bug repellent was probably safer lost than found, so I carried on until I eventually found my way back to camp.

A couple of days later (within which time I had decided that I needed the protection of clothing while hiking), I came unexpectedly upon a hut hanging on the side of a small cliff. I investigated and found that it was the hermitage of Father William, a Trappist monk who had lived in the woods for seven years, visiting his monastery about once a month for provisions and community prayer. In my clinical practice I meet a good number of social dropouts, but I had never come face to face with a genuine hermit. I was intrigued.

Father William was a responsive, sociable sort of chap in his late thirties, friendly, warm, and courteous. He was glad to see me and curious about what I was doing there—a mutual feeling that started us off on an entire day of talking together, hiking together, and praying together. I grew more and more impressed with the man as time went on, with his stability and maturity. He seemed to have accomplished in isolation what I had been trying to teach myself and my patients for years. He was open, honest, and concerned about himself and others.

I asked him how he did it. "Did what?" he asked. "Grew up," I replied. "How did you grow up?" "Oh, that's easy to explain," he said. "It wasn't easy to *do*, but it is easy to explain. Seven years ago, when I first came into these woods, I was a mixed-up kid. Perhaps I needed

141

psychotherapy more than solitude, but I knew that if I lived alone, at least I could no longer simply blame others for my plight. I still struggle with uncertainty about myself, but I have stopped fighting myself in the process. For example," he went on, "when I got frightened I used to try to hide it, or deny it, or avoid it; but now I don't. If I am afraid, I try to assess whether the danger is within me or without. If without, I try to do something about it. If it is from within, I don't ignore the feeling but allow it to build. I let it take over my whole body. Sometimes it's only about forty degrees in this hut in the winter, but I have broken out in a feverish, frightened sweat. I have been so frightened that my clothes have been soaked with perspiration. I have trembled uncontrollably. But I let it happen, even encourage it. After a while, my body relaxes and the fear subsides. Then I know that I am safe, inside and out. And I thank God for the experience. My fear still frightens me, but I don't let it destroy me any longer." I was fascinated. Here, in the middle of the woods, was a man who knew very little about academic psychology and yet had discovered on his own an effective way of dealing with his fear so that it could become a revelation and a prayer for him.

"What do you do when you get angry?" I asked. "Surely you must get angry at times." "Oh sure," Father William replied. "But I just do the same thing. I give in to the feeling. I let my imagination go. You know, I have even felt like throwing this little hut off the cliff in my anger. And like hurting myself. But I permit the feeling to overtake me, as strongly as it can. Then I decide what to do about it. It always works. I have learned to choose between what I feel like doing and what I decide is best for me . . . and for my hut," he added with a wry grin. "My anger used to terrify me; but I have learned that no matter how mad I get and for whatever reason, I don't need to strike out at myself or

142

anything or anyone else. My anger is part of me, and I thank God for it."

As good and as whole a man as Father William I have scarcely met. More than anything else, he made the week in the woods I had so long talked about before, worth talking about afterwards.

None of our natural human resources is so neglected as the ability to be alone with ourselves. We fear the tedium, the waste of time, the risk of unanswerable questions; but most of all we fear discovering that absence of self-esteem lurking just beneath the surface of our brittle, cosmetic, social selves. And so the very person most of us could least tolerate being with for more than a few minutes without something to distract or entertain us, we end up forcing on others for hours, days, even years at a time. "Thou shalt love thy neighbor as thyself," say the Scriptures. Perhaps before those words can properly be understood as a commandment, they must first be understood as a statement of fact: Like it or not, you will love your neighbor only as much as you are first capable of loving yourself.

Each of us *learns about* the wisdom of those who have gone before us long before we can *discover* it for ourselves and decide how to *appropriate* it into our lives. This book has been about a few simple and traditional ideas which are part of the story of my search for wisdom. As time and experience progress, they become fewer, simpler, and more traditional. Some day, who knows, perhaps I shall see deeply enough into the truth of our humanity and care deeply enough about its limits to live by the words of the psalmist: "May my silence be Your praise."